TOP 1% PARENTS RAISE TOP 1% CHILDREN

LEARN THE SECRETS TO RAISING TOP 1% CHILDREN

TOP 1% PARENTS RAISE TOP 1% CHILDREN

LEARN THE SECRETS TO RAISING TOP 1% CHILDREN

HUNI HUNFJORD

Copyright © 2016 by Watchon Publishing.

Copyright © 2016 by Watchon Publishing
All rights reserved. Printed in Keflavik, Iceland.

No part of this book may be used or reproduced in any manner whatsoever without written permission from the author and/or publisher. Although the author and publisher have made every effort to ensure that the information in this book was correct at press time, the author and publisher do not assume and hereby disclaim any liability to any party for any loss, damage, or disruption caused by errors or omissions, whether such errors or omissions result from negligence, accident, or any other cause.

This book is a work of non-fiction.

For information contact:
Kirkjuvegur 28, 230 Keflavik, Iceland
phone: +354 821 1977
http://www.HuniHunfjord.com

Cover design by Huni Hunfjord
Book design, editing and formatting by ESelfpublishing Services

ISBN: 978-9935-9342-0-8
First Edition: October 2016

TABLE OF CONTENTS

WHY I WROTE THIS BOOK	1
BREAKING MENTAL BLOCKS AND CELEBRATING	7
CHAPTER 1. FINDING YOUR WHY	15
CHAPTER 2. BETTER DECISIONS, KNOW YOUR NUMBERS	23
CHAPTER 3. CHANGE DON'T WANTS INTO DESIRABLE GOALS	29
CHAPTER 4. MINDSET	37
CHAPTER 5. ANCHORING	55
CHAPTER 6. EXPECT RESULTS IN YOUR LIFE	61
CHAPTER 7. RESPONSIBILITY	77
CHAPTER 8. LAW OF ATTRACTION	89
CHAPTER 9. ALIGNMENT AND VIBRATION	115
CHAPTER 10. CHANGING YOUR TUNE AND ENERGY VIBRATION	125
CHAPTER 11. BRAIN POWER AND HEALTH	135
CHAPTER 12. SEEDS OF GRATITUDE	141
CHAPTER 13. FEELINGS ARE NEITHER RIGHT NOR WRONG	147
CHAPTER 14. FUN LESSONS	153
CHAPTER 15. RITUALS AND HABITS	163
IN CLOSING	187
ABOUT THE AUTHOR	192

WHY I WROTE THIS BOOK

Most of the schooling systems in the world sadly limit the creativity that resides within our children. The schooling is focused on teaching knowledge, while there is a great lack of teaching wisdom. The difference is that we learn many facts in school, but what good are the facts when we are not taught how to use the facts to be more creative or how to apply the knowledge to live a happy and successful life.

I finished my mandatory schooling following that education with a junior college, then university where I got my bachelor's degree in business from US, and then I graduated from post production film school in UK and finally got my master's degree in business from Iceland. Even though I had all this education I was not successful, but wanted to be. It was not until I started to learn from mentors that had achieved success in their lives, how to apply knowledge through wisdom. Each time I learned something from my mentors I always thought to myself; *"why was I not taught this when I was a child?"* My first experience from a mentor was in 2012 when I started to be coached at the Rich Dad Organization. It was literally like being pulled out of a cave I had lived in all my life and seeing the sunlight for the first time in my life. Since then I have felt that same feeling over and over again while learning how to manifest my dreams, doing mindset work, practicing the law of attraction, performing gratitude rituals and when I started to give when I did not think I could afford it amongst many other life changing methods and rituals, many of them which have become habits today.

The reason I wrote this book is to give parents the tools needed to teach their children to become limitless before the start of schooling or as soon as possible thereafter. To enable them to embrace the true creativity we are all born with and nourish it. I am not saying children should not go to school, on the contrary, I think schooling is great in many ways, but not to nurture the creativity and happiness each child should experience. That is where we, the parents, play the biggest role. I started implementing the methods on my youngest child about two years ago, when she was only 3 years old and she amazes me all the time. Children understand much more than we usually give them credit for. I want you to have the methods and rituals I wish I could have known at an early age.

I was lucky enough to have a spiritual father who taught me many positive things, like how to visualize a goal. Just by being able to close my eyes and see the thing happen in my head over and over again until it becomes real. My father also showed me things that have been some of my biggest mindset blocks in my life, like how to not ask for help and do everything myself. My parents brought me up with very little money. I realized that very young and I was always looking for ways to make money with little success.

If I could go back in time as me now and talk to my younger version, I would say; *"Look at what people, that are successful and happy, are doing and do as they, learn from them and find a mentor at an early age to become what you truly want to become."*

This book is a great start for all parents to implement simple strategies into their lives and teach their children at an early age how to manifest their dreams, how to visualize anything they want to accomplish until it is accomplished, how to start being grateful for all the things they have in their lives right now, how to take responsibility for their reality and how giving works. I did not give until it was put to me in this way – if you can't afford to give 10 cents from each dollar today, you will definitely not be able to give $10,000 out of a $100,000. The mentality of scarcity stays with you even when you start to make some money. It took a lot of courage for me to start giving when I did not think I could. It is, however, one of the vital steps to take, to be able to shift your mentality of scarcity to a mentality of abundance. I know that people who are happy are not necessarily the wealthiest, but I also know that the happiest people follow their dreams and make them come true.

This book can be used to teach our children about abundance and how to become wealthy as well, but that is not the main focus, the main focus is teaching them to realize their dreams and make them come true. A big part of being successful and living a prosperous, happy life, is not having to worry about finances. Always remember, there is a big difference between being wealthy and not having to worry about bills.

This book is the start of something great, which includes a series of lectures, practical online content and other books to come, which will give parents all the tools needed to raise the best generation yet.

I look forward, on your behalf, to the changes that lay ahead and the endless possibilities the future has to offer for you and your family.

WHY YOU SHOULD READ THIS BOOK

I truly believe and know that the methods I talk about in this book work, but what is the hidden message in the book? The hidden message is that by a parent picking this book up and starting to teach their children, they themselves will benefit the most to start with, then a little bit later their children will as well. A parent can work on personal development and include their children in the process. The book will give the family as a whole great value and give the parents, who are not already implementing personal growth strategies, the understanding, that when we work on ourselves and then teach our children the same, we really are contributing our time for our children's futures.

HOW COACHABLE ARE YOU AS A PARENT?

I want you to grade yourself, with the grade score 0 being the lowest to the score of 10 being the highest. Two questions before you read the book. What is your score on, how willing are you to learn and how willing are you to change?

If your score is very low, then you will probably waste your time reading this book. This book is designed to change lives. This book is for parents who are willing to learn and make changes in their lives. For parents who want more for their children. If you want more, then you are asking for change, because if you don't change anything, you will keep on receiving what you are already receiving in your life.

If you scored high and are willing to learn and change, then this is the right book for you. You don't have to believe anything blindly in the book. I encourage you to implement the rituals and methods and find out for yourself. I know that the rituals and methods work, but I am not asking you to believe it blindly, try it and see if your circumstances in life will not be completely different after implementing rituals until they become lifelong habits. Once a ritual becomes a habit and you start to do the habit daily without thinking about it, you become unconsciously competent. Doing the habits with ease, like walking is to most of the parents around the world, they walk around without putting much conscious effort into it. Doing the habits with ease like breathing, it becomes a part of your daily unconscious efforts.

BREAKING MENTAL BLOCKS AND CELEBRATING

Break down your blocks and start your transformation to become a better parent.

Most parents want to be better parents and seek advice from people who are successful, but often do not take any action in transforming what they need to transform to become better parents.

It is important to know why you might not have taken action before.

Many people do not know why they did not start implementing routines of success in their lives and maybe this information will help you get started.

Let's start with three questions, please only provide yes or no answers.

> Are you a parent?
>
> Do you want to become a better parent?
>
> Have you ever wanted more out of life than you have now e.g. success, career, relationship, money or anything else?

If you answered all three questions with a yes, then you are in the right place. Now one more question, but before I ask, let me tell you one thing; it takes action and some willpower to transform your life. When you answer this question, say the answer out loud as it makes it easier for you to monitor how you are truly feeling. It's very important to monitor the vibrational changes in your body when you answer. Here is the question.

> *Do you truly want to transform your life in any way, become a better parent, be better off financially, have better relationships, be happier or anything else that you would like to transform?*

If you said yes, did you notice anything? What did you notice when you answered the question out loud?

Did you get a feeling of release from the upper body; did you open up and feel very good?

If you did you are most likely already starting to transform your life in some way or already have everything you ever wanted. But maybe you had a gut feeling that what you said is true but something is not quite right. That gut feeling is one of the most important tools we are born with, to tell us if the conscious and subconscious mind is working in alignment or not. Our conscious beliefs might be the opposite of what we subconsciously truly believe, for whatever reason that might be.

If you said yes to the last question but had a gut feeling that something was off, you most likely have what is called a subconscious block. That could easily be the reason that you have not yet taken the required action in the transformation you would like to see in your life. A subconscious block is when your beliefs trigger an emotional response to a certain situation and that emotion could be fear for example. If you have already started your journey in your transformation, this method can be useful for you for other subconscious blocks that you might have or might encounter in the future.

This is one of many methods to unlock the subconscious belief that is blocking you. In this example we are going to be concentrating on those who got the gut feeling that something was not quite right, because it could possibly be the reason you have not transformed your life already, or taken the right action needed to start your transformation.

This exercise can undo the subconscious block you have and remember this can be used on any type of subconscious blocks you might have. Your subconscious belief might be that you cannot change your life, let's change that with this simple exercise.

> Please take out a piece of paper and a pen.
>
> Write this down on the paper; "*My old belief, I cannot transform my life.*"
>
> Then write the opposite statement below the first statement; "*My new true belief, I can and I will transform my life.*"

Then when you have time, find a quiet room with the lights dimmed. Turn your cell phone off and anything that can cause interruption. Now relax yourself into a meditative state, for those who meditate on a regular basis know what that is and for those who do not, this is how.

> Take deep breaths, relaxing and calming your body down and concentrate on each body part, head, face, neck, shoulders, arms, hands, chest, stomach, back, legs and feet. Focus on each body part, moving from your head to your toes and feel the relaxation when you focus on each body part.
>
> Next you calm the mind by thinking about a single word, you could use the word *"love"* for example or any other word you would like. Thinking about this one word will help your mind to relax. Those who meditate use their mantras to do the same.
>
> When you feel your mind relaxed then say the following statement out loud, as soft and effortless as possible, your ears should be able to hear it but no louder than that.

"Hi my subconscious mind.

Up until now we have been holding on to this old belief that <u>I cannot transform my life</u>.

I now realize that this belief is false. I want you to replace that old belief that <u>I cannot transform my life,</u> with this new true belief which is; <u>I can and I will transform my life.</u>

From this day forward we will replace the old false belief that I cannot transform my life, with this new true belief that I can and I will transform my life.

I want you to permanently replace this old false belief that I cannot transform my life, with this new true belief that I can and I will transform my life, permanently. Make it so now and forever!"

> Repeat that statement for 5, 10, 20 minutes or however long it will take to release you block. You will feel when this is done, when you transform the vibration of your subconscious mind there will be no doubt, you will feel it, you will know it.
>
> When this is done don't forget to thank your subconscious mind like you would thank an old friend for good advice or how you would thank someone that wants to invest in you.

If for any reason the old belief surfaces in the next two weeks, be alert and catch it right away. Say this out loud and laugh at it. *"No I don't believe that anymore now I have this new true belief that I can and I will transform my life."* This will shift your energy vibration back into alignment right then and there.

Here is the really good news, when you have done this you're halfway there.

I honestly believe that this is the case with anything we do in life. Take the first step and you are halfway there. Let's say that your subconscious block is to speak out loud and you can't do this exercise, then you will find other methods later on in the book to unblock your subconscious mind without speaking. The reason I chose this method here at the beginning, is because it works the best for me and others I know.

I want to congratulate you on completing this first step and here is a small bonus tip for you to accelerate your growth even faster using the methods in this book.

Have you ever heard of Richard Branson? Let me tell you one thing that he does and I do as well today. Each time Richard Branson has a small success of any kind he celebrates it in some way. Each time I reach a goal today, even a small success on the treadmill, I celebrate. Find something that gives you a rewarding feeling, it could be anything, like going to the movies, out for a dinner, cooking with the family, taking a drive through the countryside with the family, or simply reaching your arms up in the air like you just won the marathon at the Olympics, whatever makes you feel like a winner. Use this thing to celebrate each little win or progress you make. This will make your transition to success so much faster and so much more fun.

SUMMARY

To start taking action, we have to find what is stopping us. That reason why we have not taken action before is most often a subconscious block or in other words a belief we might not have realized we had.

Take that subconscious block, reverse it and create a new subconscious belief.

Celebrate each little victory in life. Stop and smell the roses!

THE TIME TO START YOUR TRANSFORMATION IS NOW!

CHAPTER 1. FINDING YOUR WHY

What is your why? Your why is the reason you need to transform your life. The reason you use to fuel yourself and inspire yourself to achieve anything you want.

You might have read a similar statement somewhere before, but what exactly does it mean?

> "Find your why and your what can be achieved regardless of its magnitude."
>
> Huni Hunfjord

We humans have been pushing the limitations of our bodies and minds through the ages. When a person breaks a new limit, it seems like the rest of humanity can easily follow and replicate the results. Here are two examples to explain what I mean.

The first example will describe something that we know we cannot do, or so we thought.

Until the year 1954 it was thought impossible for humans to run the mile (1,609 meters) in under four minutes. Some scientists had even published their findings, about how that was not possible due to our DNA structure and that we are simply not built to be able to run that fast. In May 1954, Roger Gilbert Bannister, was the first runner who managed to run the mile in under 4 minutes. That in itself was amazing, but what I personally think is even more amazing, is that only two months later two other runners managed to run the mile in under 4 minutes as well. When we know something is possible, it becomes much easier to accomplish.

The second example will describe something that was unknown to this one man who changed the rules so to speak.

In 1983 a potato farmer at the age of 61, won the inaugural Westfield Sydney to Melbourne Ultra marathon in Australia. This is an 875 km run. Cliff Young, the potato farmer, did not look at what other runners were doing before he ran for the first time in this race. He did not realize that everyone would run and then sleep and then run and so forth. Because he did not know that, he ran the whole time without stopping, he did not sleep at all. He ran for 5 days and 15 hours to finish the race and he broke the previous record by two days. From that day forward no one else slept in the race. The runners who ran the race after that knew that this was possible and they broke his record soon after that.

These two examples are to illustrate a point and for you to think about. If your dream or goal in life has been accomplished by anyone, before you start to work towards that goal, it means that it will be that much easier for you to achieve the same results. We continue to break our own records all the time. We know more and more about the power that we are born with inside of us, that we can use, if we know how. We all have that seed of success inside of us from birth and it is so powerful, that when it awakens you will discover success beyond your wildest dreams.

THE QUESTION IS HOW DO WE UNLEASH THAT POWER THAT IS ALREADY RESIDING WITHIN US?

There are several ways of doing that. One of the most powerful methods is to find your why, a big enough reason to do it, so that you will be working from a higher energy frequency than before. So that you find such a strong desire to finish the task at hand, that you cannot think of anything that could stop you. Big enough reason so that, no matter what someone else will tell you, it will not stop you on your way to achieving that goal or manifesting that dream. If you ask yourself why, then you have to find a big reason that fires you up, that lights you up each time you think about it. Why should you become successful, why should you do better than now, why do you want it? Does it make you feel great thinking about that goal and what it will accomplish?

Have you ever heard a story about a mother saving her child stuck under a car and she just moves the car off the child and then she can never repeat that task? Her why at that moment was so strong, so powerful, and so intense that she became superman or superwoman.

WHAT IS YOUR WHY?

One of the biggest upsets in sports history was on February 11th in 1990 when the underdog Buster Douglas, knocked out the undisputed heavyweight champion Mike Tyson. When Buster Douglas was asked what motivated him in that fight, he explained that his mother had just passed away and during her last days on earth, she told people that Douglas would win the fight. His why was so great at the time that his win became one of the biggest upsets in sports history.

I know entrepreneurs that motivate themselves in different ways. One of my friends shared with me that each morning when he wakes up and thinks about snoozing the alarm, he drives himself forward with the thought of, how many children can I save in the future from starvation? He said that if he gets up and continues to grow and succeed, he will be able to give more financial support to his cause, his why. That is very powerful, but remember, his passion is helping children, around the world, who do not have enough food. That is what drives him every day, that is his WHY. What is your WHY?

Some people say that they want to become rich and that is fine, but that is not a why. You can on the other hand use money to fulfill your why, to achieve your why. Maybe your dream is to travel the world with your family, that can be a why, but it is not a very strong why. That means, if you have set traveling the world with your family as a why, then you must work harder than anyone you have ever seen working towards their transformation in their lives. You will have to be one of the strongest, most motivated people on the planet to succeed with a why of that nature.

How can we find a bigger, better why? Is your why to solve hunger in the world, or to feed 1.000 people daily for the rest of your life? Is it to leave a legacy behind for your children, or maybe to empower other people to succeed in life? Maybe it is the legacy you want to leave for your children and you start working on that right now. In a few years or even after 20 years you succeed and have a lot of money, then you might realize that money does not mean anything, but you left a legacy behind because your children took part in your transformation and realized that they can help other people do the same. Maybe that is the greatest legacy you can give your children, to let them participate in your transformation and learn life skills that are priceless. If your why is strong enough, then the hard work will actually not feel like hard work at all. What is your why?

Are you doing anything for your children today that feels like a sacrifice? Are you working at a job that you don't like that much and tell yourself that you are doing it for your kids? If so, how's that working out for you? Do you realize that you are actually leading by example in everything you do; are you demonstrating a struggle or demonstrating that you are thriving with that decision? When you are working on your transformation towards your goals and dreams and getting your children involved you are leading by example of thriving, from day one. Are you ready to find you true why and do what you love and reap the success you deserve in your life? What is your why?

Is your why, your children? If so, then how can you motivate yourself to do the rituals, the exercises and do the work needed to succeed?

Make the decision right now, to transform your life. Make the decision to take charge and follow the rituals and methods given to you by people who have already used them to succeed. All the methods in this book are adapted from people with great success stories already. The methods are actual footprints of success made by millionaires and billionaires. Have you ever walked in heavy snow before? Do you make new tracks or do you walk in the path that successful people already made in the snow? I have a lot of experience in walking in snow and although making new tracks is fun, it is very hard if you are walking all day. Life is a marathon, not a sprint. I choose to walk in the footprints any day. Have you ever seen migrating birds fly? They use the momentum of one another to make the flight easier; why not use the momentum that has already been created in the world by successful people and make the transformation that much easier for you?

CAN YOU NAME YOUR WHY?

Can you come up with a strong why with your children? Can you and your children work towards something together, a common why? The answer is yes!

Now it is time for you to tell yourself why you want to transform your life and take action. You could find a cause that your children are interested in and use it to fuel your success story. Remember that financial goals are just one type of a goal. You could have a goal to be the greatest role model in your children's life.

> What type of person do you need to be today to become their biggest role model?

> Can you take your children and do some volunteer work in the community, can you spend time teaching others what

you know already or could you take part in their career path?

Could you set up a group that meets every week to strive towards a common goal for the neighborhood for example?

There is no limit on what your why can be. Do you want to change the world, if so, why? How does it make you feel when you think about it? The how is not so important now, the why is the most important part, because when you are driven by a strong why that makes you feel great and you are constantly thinking about the results with a great feeling, the how will reveal itself on your path.

My Why, is to create a brand that inspires parents to teach their children life skills to be able to reach their goals in life at an early age and give the parents all the tools needed to create the best generation yet.

SUMMARY

Finding your why, gives you a reason big enough to persist in your journey to succeed.

Finding a common goal to strive towards with your children, will make the journey more fun and more meaningful.

When you have found your why and if your why is strong enough, no-one can stop you, not even you.

CHAPTER 2. BETTER DECISIONS, KNOW YOUR NUMBERS

WHY DO WE NEED TO KNOW OUR NUMBERS?

What does it trigger in our mind when we write down what we consume or what we spend our money on?

Do you know where you stand today? If not, I assure you that you need to know it to be able to reach your goals. It is like planning a trip to a certain city on a map, if you don't know where your starting point is, it will be hard to plan the trip. Most people cannot tell you how much they spend on food each month, or how many calories they burn, how many calories they eat, how much quality time they spend with their children or how much money they need to be financially free, to be able to spend more time with their children.

To measure something and then measure it again, makes it possible for us to tell if we are going in the right direction, doing it right or not, if a person is growing or slowly dying. Whatever the goal you have in mind for yourself as a parent or for your children, it will be very hard to know when you have reached it, if you don't know where you stand today and where you want to be. Sometimes goals can be measured without knowing where you are at today, these goals are the exception to the rule and we still need to know our numbers during our journey, to know when we have arrived.

For example, if your goal would be to make $10,000 per month, you need to know what you make each month and each week on your journey there. When you reach your goal of $10,000 per month, you might find out that this goal did not solve what you thought it would. It might not be enough to make you financially free. For you to be able to set a realistic goal knowing that when you reach it, it will solve your problem, you need to first know what you need to succeed right now. That is why I consider setting your goals, knowing your numbers, where you stand now and where you need to stand to reach your goals to be a better way. When we finally reach our goals, we always need to have a new goal ready, the next goal! That will help you sustain your goal and to grow even further.

It is totally up to you if you want to set a goal now and find out when you reach the goal if it was great enough for you or not. I will always recommend that you know where you stand now and based on that information you make a decision on how much or what you need, to be able to solve the problem. This applies to almost all the goals we set in life.

When we start to monitor the things we do today, we write them down. The secret about writing down what you do is so much more than just knowing what you do, let me explain. Let me tell you what writing these things down, does for a human being. I am going to use two examples to illustrate this point.

1. Writing down what you consume and how much you consume.

2. Keeping a simple spending diary by writing down what you purchase, marking if it is necessary or unnecessary.

FOOD DIARY

Let's start with the food diary. When we start to write down all the things that we consume, we are doing so much more than just writing it down. We can go to several free websites and get the nutritional values from our consumption and get the facts about how many vitamins we are consuming. How much of the essential minerals, vitamins, sugars and fats we really need, that is in our current diet. We also get a list of all the crap that we are consuming, the surplus sugar amount and the types of fats we consume (including partial hydrogenation fats).

Hydrogenated fats are unnatural fats that are terrible for your health.

Three general types of fats in foods are; *Saturated* (e.g., butter, lard) - *Monounsaturated* (e.g., olive or canola oils) and *Polyunsaturated* (e.g., omega-6 oils like sunflower or safflower oil, or omega-3 oils like fish and flaxseed oils). Hydrogenation (or, more accurately, partial hydrogenation, as the process is incomplete) is the forced chemical addition of hydrogen into omega-6 polyunsaturated oils to make them hard at room temperatures, primarily used as a cheaper and less perishable substitute for butter and you should avoid it if at all possible.

This part of the food diary is the obvious part of keeping a food diary. We get the facts, but what else happens in our brain when we keep a diary like that? We start to be aware of what we are actually consuming and therefore immediately start to make better decisions when we are deciding what we consume. Some might make better decisions because they don't want a negative score in their diary, some might do it because they don't want to have a written proof anywhere of how unhealthy their diet actually is, some might do it because they just really want to eat healthy and some might have some other reason for changing his or her consumption patterns that is triggered by starting to write everything down in the food diary. The bottom line is, the reason does not matter, what matters is that you have already begun to change your life the minute you decided to start writing down what you consume!

SPENDING DIARY

The type of spending diary I recommend is to keep it as simple as possible. I recommend not listing every single object, at least not to start with. I know some of the dominant left brained people would like to list everything down, but that is overkill and not the point. The most important part of the spending diary is to write down whether your purchase was necessary or unnecessary. Example;

Date	What	Amount	Un/Necessary
01/04	Walmart groceries	$212	N
02/04	Beer at Pub	$15	U
05/04	Parking - New York	$20	N
07/04	Doctor - St Mayr's	$80	N
09/04	Donuts - Dunkin Donuts	$12	U
09/04	Movies - Goonies	$28	U
09/04	White wine & Pizza - The Hut	$74	U

The main reason why I suggest doing this as simple as possible is so you will continue doing this and to start making changes in your spending behaviors right away. Over 90% of people, who go into all the details right away, quit during their first month of writing in their spending diary.

This kind of diary does similar things for you as the food diary. You will be able to see what you are actually spending your money on, how much you spend on groceries and so forth. You are forced each time to think about, if this is something that is necessary or unnecessary and you will start making better decisions right away.

Let's say you are improving your life on many levels and you decide you only need to start putting aside extra $50 dollars on top of what you're already putting aside each month, but you have no idea where to find that money. After monitoring your spending, you will find the $50 extra you need in your spending diary. By making a decision to start writing down everything you spend money on and if it is necessary or unnecessary, you have already started the transformation. By starting a spending diary you have already shifted your mindset and focus towards finding the unnecessary spending and changing it.

Start each month by calculating on another page all the things you spent money on last month and sum together all the things you considered to be necessary versus all the things you considered unnecessary.

This can be implemented and applied to anything you want to achieve. You can write down each day how you feel and set a goal of how you want to feel. You can write down how much quality time you spend with your children and how much time you would like to spend with your children. Only our imagination limits what we can monitor and what goals we set for our lives and our children's lives.

SUMMARY

Writing down what we spend our money on, helps us shift our spending habits and we can move towards our financial goals.

Writing down what we consume will shift our eating habits towards our health goals.

Writing down what we do and how we do it, gives us a clear picture of where we are today and makes it easier for us to monitor our progress while reaching our goals.

CHAPTER 3. CHANGE DON'T WANTS INTO DESIRABLE GOALS

Sometimes we have to look at the things we don't want, to find what we really want. We can take statements of what we do not want and turn them into desirable goals.

It is kind of funny when we think about it, sometimes we do something in life just because we did not want the opposite. That does not mean it was necessarily the right decision for us. You might have decided to always have ice cream available after each dinner at your house for the kids, just because you never did as a kid, but that does not necessarily make it the right thing to do. You might have decided to have ice cream available and without realizing it you were in a way criticizing how you parents raised you. You just wanted to do the opposite, meaning you were not happy with being raised to not having ice cream available.

Sometimes we might avoid something like a pothole in the road but we get our rims scratched on the sidewalk instead. Sometimes, trying to avoid something, doesn't necessarily mean a happy ending. You might decide to never implement something because it happened to you as a child and you did not like it then. For example, never to force your children to eat vegetables, but that does not mean that it is the right thing to do.

LET'S LOOK AT SOME EXAMPLES OF HOW TO CHANGE THOSE OPPOSITES INTO A POSITIVE GOAL?

What do you not want out of life? You don't want to die poor. You don't want your children to become failures when they grow up. You don't want to fail as a parent. You don't want to always have to say no, just because you can't afford it.

These are common and valid reasons to be willing to transform your life and start attracting positive results in your life. Yet at the same time this is probably one of the worst ways to think about it if you truly are striving for better results in your life. **Because what we concentrate on, grows**. If, for example, we are always thinking about that we don't want to be poor or that we wish to have no money problems, then the current results will continue to show up and even grow further in your life. The statements in your mind would look like this;

"I don't want to be poor."

"I wish I had no money problems."

However the true message we are sending to our subconscious mind is this;

"I want to be poor."

"I wish I had money problems."

Our subconscious mind does not understand *"no"*, *"not"* **or** *"don't"*, **only pure statements**. That is why we have to turn those statements into the opposites to create a good positive goal to strive for.

Let's change these two statements into a positive goal.

What is the opposite of poor? We can use wealth, being rich or abundance for example. How can we think about that same statement positively? *"I want to be wealthy."* Great job so far, but we are not done yet! Let me explain why. If you want something, then that desire is already true, yes you want it but does that mean you will get it? No, not necessarily. So let's change the same statement even more so that our subconscious mind understands it the right way to attract the desired results. Change it so your belief can start us off on that journey, right away. Change your want to will. *"I will be wealthy."* You have the same meaning in the sentence as we started with, but it will have the effect on you and your mind to move towards the price. The positive energy you work with in the statement; *"I will be wealthy"*, is going to amaze you. We will cover other examples as well and turn them into a statements that our subconscious mind will help us manifest.

Now let's change the other statement the same way. *"I wish I had no money problems."* What is the opposite of having money problems? Yes, abundance or wealth or riches. First let's start by taking the wish part out, because it works the same way as wanting does in the previous example. Yes you wish for it but does that mean you will get it? No, not necessarily. Because wanting and wishing is already true. You already want it and you already wish it, but that does not mean you will. It's much more powerful to use *"will"* in these statements because it leaves no doubt, you will get it or you will do it. Next let's take the word problem out. Now we can say; *"I will have money"* or *"I love money"* or even; *"I am getting richer by the minute."* These will all work as an opposite of *"I wish I had no money problems."*

From now on when you think about problems or not wanting something, ask yourself how you can turn this into a direct desirable goal statement and how you can put it in a positive way so that you can start manifesting the goal or dream into your life right away. We do not have to know how it will happen, only that it will happen. Some people get stuck on the how and stop there, when most of the time your how will be revealed to you as you start to manifest the goal into your reality. Your how will most likely be something you do not know today, but might know tomorrow or the day after that.

To explain what I mean, I will use the example of a man that stands still, facing west and stares straight forward. He decides to travel east. When he knows where he wants to go (his goal) then he realizes that he must turn his head to face the direction he wants to head towards. When he turns his head he sees his how. It could be a car or a horse that was sitting outside his peripheral vision when he set his goal. The only thing he needed to know was that he was going to travel east, for example. He did not know how, when he decided that he was going east, but as soon as he set his goal and he turned his head, his how appeared. He had no doubt about his goal, the only thing he did not know, was how he was going to travel east. This is a very simple example how manifesting something works.

When you think about what will happen as a result of that goal, do it with a good feeling as it has already happened, the joyful feeling of already reaching that new state of being or goal. The happier you feel when thinking about your goal as it has already happened now, the more you magnify the manifestation power of your subconscious mind and the faster you will manifest the goal into your reality. With positive emotions, you raise your energy frequency and the higher your energy frequency is while manifesting, the more powerful your manifestation abilities become.

We will go into much more detail on how to use language to manifest and create positive energy, when we talk about alignment and vibration later in the book.

HERE IS AN EXERCISE YOU CAN DO WITH YOUR CHILDREN IF THEY KNOW HOW TO WRITE

If your child keeps on telling you that he/she can't do something, it will become their reality. You can tell your child to write the word *"can't"* on a piece of paper. Have them write it on that same piece of paper as many times as you think is necessary to implement the results. You tell your child that we are going to get rid of that word and never use it again. When the child has written the word *"can't"* multiple times, go outside and find a place you can safely light the paper of fire, if you have a grill in the back, that is the perfect place to implement this strategy.

Explain to your child that what you are about to do is to make that word disappear from their life. Place the paper on the grill and light it on fire. Then just watch as it disappears. A parent shared this exercise with me and said it worked like a charm, her son never used the word *"can't"* again. This action is very visual and the child understands that this piece of paper is gone; it has been burnt up and will not return into their life. You can also bury the paper in the yard if you don't want to burn it, it gives the same results.

Another example of implementing the strategy of not using the word *"can't"* is the story of Jennifer Bricker who was born without legs. She was adopted and the only thing her foster-parents decided from day one was to never allow her to use the word *"can't."* When she was really young all she wanted was to become a gymnast. Her parents had to support her in any way possible so she would live up to their number one rule, not using the word *"can't."* After she became an adult, she made a living as an acrobat and aerialist. Thanks to the simple rule of not using can't, she was and still is, when this is written, as unlimited as you and your children should always be.

SUMMARY

Turn the things you don't want, into a direct desirable goal and you can achieve anything you desire.

If we stop using words like *"can't"*, we live without limits, or even better if you teach your children from day one, never to limit themselves by using words like *"can't"*, they can achieve all their goals in life.

CHAPTER 4. MINDSET

SHIFT YOUR MINDSET TO REACH YOUR GOALS

The work involved in changing or shifting your mindset is not simply to be able to do or achieve something; it is so much more than that. The work you put into changing our mindset will change your reality. Shifting your mindset is taking your goals and matching your energy vibration to those goals then snapping into alignment with your goals by experience the emotions of completion or success before it happens.

Have you ever thought to yourself that you were meant for greatness? Ever thought that you should be doing more? Ever thought that your message to the world is powerful and you should be influencing millions?

Let's start with the basics, what are your goals? Let's use the goal of becoming financially free to illustrate the groundwork and rituals needed to shift your mindset and start manifesting that goal into you life. Many people say their goal is to have more money. That is a very unspecified goal and therefore is not going to get you far, because if you would find a dollar bill lying on the street right now, then you have already achieved your goal, you have more. It is important to know what becoming financially free means to you. There are two options to start with, either you can set your goal as an estimated fixed amount or you can do some calculations to find the exact amount you need to be able to choose to stop working if you want to. In this example we will use an estimated fixed amount of $10,000 per month. Your goal is to earn $10,000 each month. The first steps you take when working on your mindset is to ask yourself a few questions.

"Am I worth $10,000 a month?" If your answer is no, then you need to use another amount you truly believe you are worth. Repeat the question for as long as it takes, until you are confident answering with a yes. When you answer yes, regardless of the amount, then you can start working with that goal. You can increase the amount later.

Start by writing down 20 reasons why you are worthy of this goal. Writing it down will help you manifest your true belief about your self-worth. It will also help you eliminate self-doubt. Stop reading the book here for a minute, take out a piece of paper and write 20 reasons, why you are worthy of this goal. I don't want you to just read through the book without doing anything, unless you are planning to start at the beginning again as soon as you finish reading it the first time and then implementing the methods and rituals from the book.

HOW CAN YOU CHANGE YOUR MINDSET TO BE ABLE TO REACH YOUR GOAL?

First you have to think about the person you will become when you are making $10,000 per month? Are you any different from who you are today?

What do you wear?

Do you have a new haircut?

Are you giving to charity? If so, how much and to what charity?

How do you talk to people?

How do you walk?

How do you think?

How do you act?

What are people saying about you?

What does it feel like when you think about the person you will become, once you reach your goal?

Ask yourself as many questions as you can about the person you will become and write it down. Once you have all the details, you need to start acting exactly like the person you have described, right now, TODAY! This is a crucial step in changing your mindset and alignment to manifest your goals. You must start to act like the person you will become and not the other way around. You don't reach your goal and then become that person. Shift into that identity now, obtain your goal and then sustain your goal.

Next step is to list down the things you can possibly do to get closer to your goal.

- ✧ You could decide to get a mindset coach, like I did. My first mindset coach Regan Hillyer is a fantastic coach. My experience with a mindset coach is kind of like being pulled out of a dark cave and seeing the sunlight for the first time. That is how strong the change can be with a mindset coach.

- ✧ By reading this book you are off to a great start to your mindset work.
- ✧ You could also get a writing coach to help you write a book.
- ✧ You could get a life coach.
- ✧ You could register for an online course where other people like yourself are starting out and sharing their journey together with you.
- ✧ You could form a mastermind group where people share their ideas and help each other to reach the goals by sharing their story, wins and losses. This could be as simple as creating a Facebook group for like minded individuals sharing their journey together.

Whatever your action plan is, you must include time for a morning ritual and time to feed the brain. You feed the brain by reading or listening to people who have already achieved your desired goals, learn from them and implementing their ideas into your journey. You want to be a great parent; therefore you need to define what makes a parent great. You have to find people who you consider good parents and learn from them. What makes them good parents? Can you do the same?

You also need to start thinking about the success, the finish line, the prize. When you reach your goal how will your household, your health and your life change? How will your children change and your career change? How will you feel?

When you think about the answers to these questions, think about them as the changes have already happened; experience that great feeling you are striving towards, right now!

WHY IS IT SO IMPORTANT TO VISUALIZE AND FEEL THOSE EMOTIONS WHILE ASKING THESE QUESTIONS?

One of the reasons is because of your co-pilot, fear! Fear is real and fear is always going to stay with you. Fear has been a natural thing for humankind for survival. The more successful you become, the stronger and bigger your co-pilot becomes. It is totally up to you if you let him come in the front of the car or if you let him ride as a passenger in the back. I recommend the backseat, since fear is a very poor driver. Fear is an emotional response. It's a response to a belief you have adopted at some point in your life. In this case it could be fear of success. The fear itself has no meaning or value other than as an indicator. Let's not work on our fears because they're a symptom, they're not a cause. We always need to work on the cause and the cause is always a belief. You need to reprogram your beliefs. Although fear will always be a part of us, you need to constantly be looking for the reason behind the different types of fear or in other words, what belief do you have that is triggering fear. You need to identify the beliefs you have, that are causing the fear and change them. This is an ongoing progress through life, because with every new circumstance or every win in life, new fears will emerge. The question is how ca you identify the trigger and change your beliefs. We will cover that a bit later in this chapter.

Here is a list of common fears that hold people back from success.

- Fear of criticism
- Fear of poverty (being stuck in survival mode)
- Fear of old age (and death)
- Fear of failure
- Fear of offending others
- Fear of looking foolish
- Fear of success

Have you ever self-sabotaged something in your life? A relationship, career, your health, or something else? Was it at a point when you already reached a goal or when you were close to reaching that goal? Did you suddenly do something that sabotaged the results you had achieved? It could be a relationship, your career or your body, for example. The cause is almost always some type of fear. That is why it is important for you to have the next goal ready before you reach the first goal, let me explain. You are working with the goal of making $10,000 per month and you reach that goal in 10 months from now. Then you could easily self-sabotage the results and have to start all over again, it could repeat itself indefinitely. The cause of this would be your fear jumping in the front seat and taking control. What steps can you take to avoid this and keep the fear in the back seat?

You should prepare by thinking about what will happen when you reach your initial goal and already have the next goal set! It's that simple!

If you don't have your next goal ready and your income keeps growing, you are headed into the unknown without a plan. It would be like sailing a boat to the end of the world and falling off the end; we don't know what is beyond that point, the space of the unknown, in which fear takes control and let me emphasize that fear is a lousy pilot! I just want to mention that the end of the world is a metaphor just in case you were wondering. You must think about, feel and decide what you will do when reaching your goal, to be able to sustain it. Warren Buffet is a great example of learning to live with the fear, keeping it in the back seat. He went to a Dale Carnegie seminar, not to learn to speak without having his knees shake, but to learn to speak while they were shaking! You need to eliminate the space of the unknown from the equation by visualizing how you will handle reaching the initial goal and where you are heading from there.

HAVE YOU BEEN ON THE ROAD TO SUCCESS BEFORE BUT NEVER QUITE REACHED THE DESIRED OUTCOME, NO MATTER WHAT YOU HAVE TRIED?

If that is the case, then you might have a fear that is triggered by a belief you have, also called a subconscious block, that prevents you from advancing or causes you to self-sabotage the current results. If you have not identified what it is, then it is very important to start looking at what belief is triggering that fear. When you realize what the trigger is that is stopping you, you can change it. Your block might be the belief that you will have to do it all on your own. I use this example here because it was my biggest subconscious block triggering my fear of success. I will use this example to illustrate the method of releasing, finding the origin and changing the decision I made in the past that created this block. Why do you believe that you will have to do it all on your own? Could it be because you are an introverted person? Can you identify when you created this block? Can you think about when you started to believe that you will have to do it on your own? You might remember that we already covered one method to unlock the subconscious mind. We did that in an earlier chapter by talking out loud to our subconscious mind.

Here is another way to deal with this and we can use this method to identify where this block was created in your mind and you can release the block with this method as well. While walking you through this method I share with you how I found my block, believing that I should do everything myself.

FIND YOUR BLOCK, CHANGE THE DECISION AND START TO REAP THE BENEFITS TODAY

Everything starts with a decision and a belief.

When you make a decision, you start thinking about what and how. You start implementing this in your daily life and it can become your block even though you do not realize it at the time. Surely you did not make an aware decision to form a block, but you decided something that created the block and you need to find what decision that was. In this example the belief of you having to do it all on your own is what is stopping you. You need to find what created this limited belief and when it was created. It could be a limited belief of self-doubt. In my case I decided to belief that I should do everything myself. My limited belief was created from my upbringing. I was raised in a home with both my parents. My father, who is a perfectionist, can't have anyone do anything for him, because he believes that no one can do the job as well as he can. There is no question that he is very talented, but at the same time he will take four times longer to complete a task because it has to be perfect.

At what point in my life did I decide to start believing that I will have to do everything myself? I developed some talents from my father, I became very good at solving problems, creating, and building things. In taking after my father I started re-creating his patterns from being raised by a man that never accepted any assistance and therefore self-sabotaging my success.

The following is an illustration of how you can find the source and release your subconscious block, using my block as an example. You can implement this method on anything else you might recognize as your subconscious block triggering fear on your path to success. How can you change that one decision, your limited belief, you want to change?

First identify and write down what decision you want to change. Using my example, you would write; *"I want to change the decision I made to believe that I have to do everything myself."*

Next find a nice quiet place, sit comfortably and use the subconscious timeline, as described below, to change that decision

Using this method you start by closing your eyes, taking one hand and pointing it towards what you FEEL is your past. Then take your other hand and point it towards your future. It doesn't matter where the hands are pointing, your timeline does not need to be straight. What matters is that you have both hands pointing somewhere simultaneously so that you can visualize both your past and your future.

With your eyes still closed visualize the imaginary line from your past to your future and imagine yourself hovering about 2,5 m (8ft) above the *"now"* on your timeline, feeling both your past and your future.

Start floating backwards into your past, you might catch glimpses, see some images, or even hear, smell or feel something, just keep on floating, observing and enjoy what you experience. The experience of the subconscious timeline is different for everyone.

Next float forward to the *"now"* where you started, then continue floating into your future, the same thing applies as before, you might see, hear, or feel something. You are getting used to your timeline and seeing how it works.

Finally float back to the *"now"* on your timeline, once you are back slowly come down and open your eyes.

You only do this one time, to get a feel for your timeline and to get to know how you can use it to access your subconscious mind's past and future. How people see their timeline varies, some might see filing cabinets, others a forest, and others something totally different. It doesn't matter what you see, it will work just like you see it, so there is no need for you to try and change that

Now you are ready to do the exercise and change the decision you subconsciously made in the past. Since you are reading this you will obviously not be able to close your eyes while reading it (author chuckles). May I suggest using your phone or any other recording device to record yourself reading the following text, then close your eyes and play the recording back or simply read through it and then do the exercise once you've read all the way through.

> Close your eyes and hover over the *"now"* on your timeline. Think about how old you were when you made the decision to belief that you need to do everything yourself. Your subconscious mind will know right away so you shouldn't have to give it a lot of thought.
>
> Once you have the answer you are ready to start changing that decision. *(My answer came very fast to me and I knew I was around 4 or 5 years old when I saw my father building a new kitchen where we were living at the time.)*
>
> Next move towards your past and start floating towards the time period where you made that decision. You might hear see or feel things, even smell something, but don't worry if you don't, it still works, we all experience this in a different

way. *(When I was doing my timeline exercise I saw glimpses from my past as I visualized myself traveling towards my past to the first memory I had of my father building something by himself.)*

When you reach the exact point on your timeline where the decision was made, hover right above it, look down and come down towards it. Ask your subconscious mind to notice how many other options are available at that point in time. You did not have to make that decision, see how many other decisions could have been made right then and there.

When you see what options you have, go ahead and pick one new decision that will offer a better result in your future. *(I saw my situation with different eyes this time and I decided to see that my father could have done his work faster and more efficient with the help of others and therefore I decided that I would have other people help me in my future when I needed to create or build something.)*

Once you have made a new decision, float up and hover above the event facing the *"now."* Start floating towards the *"now"* watching for at least three events on your timeline that have changed, three things that actually shifted because you have now made a better decision in the past, removing your limited belief. Notice the changes that occur within you all the way from that time in the past until now. *(I noticed several times on my timeline where I had done something on my own, had changed to involving friends and family in the projects, sharing the load and success with them.)*

When you reach the *"now"* on your timeline again with your new decision, come back down and slowly open your eyes, knowing that you have now made a new decision in your past.

When you open the eyes this time, write down on the paper the new decision that you made in your past on your timeline. Once you have your new decision written down, you need to test if it is done or not. *I wrote; "I believe that I will hire people and I will get partners to help me succeed."*

Close your eyes again and go into your past on your timeline to the point where the original decision, which was blocking you, was made. Look at the event with the new decision and see if it is unchanged or if you see a new better outcome. That is the reason you chose a new decision, to have better results both in your past and your future, right?

Float back to *"now"* on your timeline, still hovering above. You are going to test this out in your future, go to any unspecified date in the future and see how this new decision impacts your results. Just stay there and see how it has changed you and your outcome. See what kind of people are helping you, see how people who are smarter than you are on your team, see how you are now a part of a team and by no means are you doing things yourself any more.

Come back to *"now"*, come down to your timeline and back into the room, open your eyes when you are ready.

In doing this exercise myself I saw the possibilities of working with people, entrusting others, and I was excited about it. During the next three months I hired over 70 contractors to do small things in my life. I hired contractors to do graphic design work for me, dance choreographers, 3D modelers, 3D animators, singers, songwriters, website developers and more. I accomplished more in those three months than I did the previous 12 months.

All can be overcome by putting the fear in the back seat of the car, so to speak. You can use the timeline method to find why you have this fear and when you decided to let the fear in the front seat of your car! Once you have identified where, when and why, you can change it. You can shift your mindset.

Remember that this method can be used for any subconscious blocks, I only used my experience as an example to illustrate this method.

WHAT CHANGES DO YOU NEED TO MAKE IN YOUR LIFE TO ENSURE SUCCESS?

Who do you have to let go off in your life, what people are holding you back, what people are a negative influence? How do you think you'll manage to make your life positive while keeping the people who have negative influence around? What do you need to change to prepare for success, today? What are you worth? How many clients do you deserve? Do you deserve all the success you dream of? Is there anything about your goals that you do not believe you can achieve? These are good questions to ask yourself to see if there are other subconscious decisions from your past still blocking you.

Here are some mindset exercises that will help you rapidly manifesting the results you desire into your life.

Step into the identity right now, the identity of who you need to be to be successful or a better parent. What does it feel like when you have reached the goal? Try to stop a few times each day and take 20-30 seconds to think about and feel your success like it's already there. This will keep your positive energy flow ongoing and stop any negative energy vibrations, allowing you to experience your success like you have already achieved it.

Get into the state of knowing it already happened. Write down how you feel when you achieved it, what are people asking you, who are you thanking for your success, what are people saying about you? How do you feel? Remember that your mindset is only growing when you are out of your comfort zone, when you are challenging your current reality.

On a piece of paper write down the things you are grateful for in your future when your success is obtained. Write down as many things as you can think of and write them as you have already reached your goal, write it out as an affirmation. *"I am so happy and grateful for …. now that I have achieved ….."*

Write out your best case scenario and worst case scenario about what could possibly happen when you follow your dream and work on reaching your goals. Your worst case scenario could be for example that you will still be doing everything by yourself, or that you have lost all the money you earned and your residual income drops back to status quo. Knowing the worst case scenario really takes away all the doubt whether you should actually put in the effort to obtain your goal or not. Best case scenario, you have an awesome partnership or an awesome team and you exceed your goals. You are not worried about exceeding your goals because you already put in the work having the next goal ready and being able to sustain the success, even handling too much success.

Use the pleasure motivators to rewards yourself with each win, small or big, along the way and each new milestone you reach. What are your pain motivators, how can you punish yourself if you don't stay on track? Could you for example push yourself in the gym, extra hard? Could you take something and put it on hold until you reach the next milestone, like dining out or going to the movies? Make sure that your pain motivators are aligned with your goals, taking out TV time for example, will free up more time to work on your goals. Come up with pain and pleasure motivators to use on your journey, to reward yourself. Find out what motivates you more, pleasure or pain motivators.

One story that I really like about manifesting results into your life is the story about Jim Carrey. In 1990 he wrote a check to himself for $10,000,000 *"for acting services rendered"*, he dated the check 5 years into the future. He folded the check and put it in his wallet and kept it there. In 1995 right before Thanksgiving, his career had really taken off and he reached his desired goal. He had just signed a contract for $10,000,000 for the part in Dumb and Dumber. He exceeded that goal even further after that point.

I remember at 15 years old, having just started playing basketball, but as tall as I was, or about 191 cm (approx. 6´3) I was struggling to dunk the basketball. I had a talk with my father and told him I really wanted to be able to dunk the basketball, at the time I could only do that with a smaller ball. My father did not know anything about basketball, but asked me if I could close my eyes and see myself dunking. I said yes. Then he asked me if I could see how my feet moved, how my hands moved and how high I was jumping. I replied that I could. He then told me to visualize that into my reality, he taught me to change my mindset, how to manifest. Each night when I was in bed before I would go to sleep, I was supposed to visualize myself dunking the basketball over and over again until I fell asleep. I did that for a whole year, each night. I practiced in the gym during the day and visualized it at night.

One year later I could dunk the basketball really easily and I entered into my first televised dunk contest at the age of sixteen.

SUMMARY

Shift your mindset to reach your goals.

If you have fear of success, find what is triggering the fear and change it.

Fear is only a trigger from a belief you decided to have, so don't concentrate on the fear but instead only on the source and change it.

Visualize your goals and you will achieve them much faster.

Experience the emotions of already having achieved your goals.

Step into the identity right now, the identity of who you need to be when you have already reached your goals.

Use your subconscious timeline exercise to identify your subconscious blocks and when you decided to adapt this limiting belief that has been triggering your fears and holding you back from your success. Make a new decision, a new belief and start reaping the benefits today.

CHAPTER 5. ANCHORING

ANCHORING YOUR STATE OF MIND IS EASY AND A VERY POWERFUL TOOL YOU CAN DEVELOP

Neuro-linguistic programming is a technique used to trigger an emotional state of mind. You can, for example, use this method to stay calm in situations where you could not before. You can trigger a state of calmness even under stressful circumstances.

Anchors can appear in many forms and we all have them, whether you know it or not, examples of these are our involuntary triggers, like when you smell something and a memory comes to you, or when you hear a special song and it takes you back in time or makes you happy. What many are not aware of is that these triggers can be developed by other means, for example by touch. You can develop an anchor by pressing on your knuckle for example, what you want it to trigger, is up to you. You can use anchors to reset your state of mind. You can also create anchors in your children. One example of how to do this, is by holding both of your children's hands each time you tell them good news. By doing this consistently they will start feeling the excitement and happiness as soon as you hold their hands, before you even speak, after a few times of doing this.

I refer to this action as activating the anchor after having permanently conditioned it.

Your mood and emotions are triggered by anchors; by sight, sound, smell, touch, or actions. Sometimes you might think that your mood changes by coincidence but it is almost always triggered by some kind of an anchor. One of the things you can start to monitor, after realizing this, is what your anchors are and changing them. If you realize for example that a touch triggers you to become moody, you can learn what touch it is and you can undo that anchor. Let´s say for example that you realize having your hair touched by someone shifts your state of mind into negative vibration or a bad mood. Knowing this anchor and working with it enables you to develop a new better state of mind when your hair is being touched. Let's look at how you can create new anchors or undo a bad anchor, the same method applies for both.

Let´s use the feeling of happiness to illustrate how to create an anchor.

Think about a time in your life when you were very happy, really happy. When you have located that memory, step into that memory and try to experience the emotions that you felt then and there, again. What did you see? What did you feel? What did you hear? Was there any touch involved in the memory? What did you smell?

If you have a hard time finding a truly happy memory you can do it through the experience of your children, for example. You can think about a time when they were very happy and your empathy for your children gives you the chance to experience their happiness at that moment.

You will have to decide how you are going to anchor this feeling of happiness. You can use a mental image of something. You can use a phrase you say inside yourself to trigger it, example; *"I am so happy right now"* or basically anything you choose to use. You can also use a kinesthetic anchor, which is a point on your body you press to trigger that feeling. You could, for example, grab your wrist and squeeze it to activate the anchor. You could also combine sounds, visuals and kinesthetics to anchor that feeling. You can also use whistling as an anchor; whistling the same song to trigger the emotion of happiness. You have many ways to anchor yourself, but you must select the one you feel will work the best for you.

Here is the list of things you need to do to create your anchor, and remember you can anchor any state of mind. To illustrate this I will use the same example as before, the feeling of happiness.

Decide what you want to anchor, like happiness for example.

Choose the anchoring method you want to implement; visual, sound, touch, or a combination of these together.

Recall a memory of happiness. If you don't have a dear memory then visualize it. Once you have a vivid image in your mind and you are experiencing the state of happiness, activate the anchor, for example grabbing your wrist and squeezing it.

When the feeling or experience starts to fade release your anchor. You don't want to anchor the state of happiness fading away.

Distract your attention to something completely different to reset your mind; sing a song, close your eyes and count to ten, or anything else that works for you. Repeat the process from the beginning several times, as many times as needed.

Once you think you are ready to test the anchor, activate it and see if you can shift your state of mind to happiness.

When you have completed the tasks above, it is time to test the anchor at a point where you are not feeling happy and want to trigger happiness. If the trigger is not working you need to start over again. This means your anchor is not strong enough yet. If it is working make sure you test it out the next day to see if you have successfully created a permanent anchor.

Once you have successfully created a desired anchor you can teach your children how to or if your children are very young you can actually create the anchors, like I described above with the good news by touch for example. This is a very powerful tool for you to use in your life. Successful people I know use this method, for example when they speak at events, to trigger the emotional state of mind that they desire while sharing their message. They trigger a state of being energetic and positive, and to keep the momentum going they continue to activate the trigger while on stage.

Do you remember when you were about to go on your first exciting flight to a new country and you felt like a child before Christmas? Remember how your stomach was filled with butterflies, you were so excited. You can create an anchor for that feeling and use it when you meet new people for example. Can you imagine how much fun it would be to meet you in that state of mind?

One anchor I created by accident with my youngest child is when I am about to do something fun and exciting I always start with these words; *"Hey, I have an idea..."* I did not notice it until she started to use the same phrase when she was about to tell me anything she considered fun and exciting. When she uses the words; *"Hey, I have an idea..."* she lights up with excitement before she can tell me what it is and I do as well, because we both know that the idea she is about to share is something fun.

SUMMARY

Create an anchor to shift your state of mind or emotion.

Create anchors for your children to shift their state of mind.

Use your anchors whenever you feel the need to and keep yourself in a positive state of vibration and in alignment with your goals in life.

CHAPTER 6. EXPECT RESULTS IN YOUR LIFE

When you expect results, your mind looks for ways to achieve that searching out all the small things that will help you to attract those results.

A first impression is very important, do you agree? You have most likely heard it before. You might also have heard that you will not get a second chance to make a great first impression. Is the first impression really as important as it is said to be and why?

Most of us have met someone we did not like at first but getting to know that person we changed our minds, we might even love that person today. Many of us have also met people we really liked, even completely fell for, at first at first impression, but after getting to know them we didn't like them at all. Have you ever looked at someone you have known for some time, and thought, how did I see that person when we had our first impression? In my experience it is virtually impossible to remember what exactly we saw at first, regardless if we like or dislike that person today.

First impressions are very important if you are in a situation where you know you only have one chance to impress, for example, in a job interview or when presenting your ideas to an investor. You can be at an event, trying to network with people and you know that you'll never see some of the people you meet there again, while others you will. When you meet a person you are trying to get to invest in you or your ideas, you expect certain things to happen. You have ideas in your mind before the meeting on how the introduction will go. This is what we call expectations.

When I was learning about how to approach business minded people, I was warned that if I do not make a great first impression I would most likely lose out on an opportunity, because the investors or possible future partners, are all expecting not to do business with me. I was told they are all looking for any reason not to do business with me, and that is why my first impression must be great. JT Foxx, the world's number one Wealth Coach, says that you only have 29 seconds to impress someone and that is why you need a perfect 29 second pitch to win investors over.

What about you, what are you expecting when you approach a possible investor, a possible future mate or a new neighbor? Are you expecting him/her to do business with you? Do you expect the mate to be what you have been looking for? Do you expect the neighbor to become one of your close friends in the future? Well, if you don't, then you need to change your expectations from now on. Because if you expect them not to do business with you, not to like you, not to become your friend, they and you will look for any reason not to do just that and most likely you will both find that reason.

WHAT HAPPENS TO IN OUR REALITY WHEN WE START TO EXPECT RESULTS IN EVERYTHING WE DO?

We start to look at the world with a different mindset. We start to ask ourselves the right questions and we start to attract desires and expected results into our lives. If you go into a meeting expecting results, your mind will be wide awake for all the signs of making that reality come true. What about when you meet new people at your children's school, what are you expecting? How does your mindset change when you start to expect better results in your life? What happens when you open your mind and eyes, for the best possible outcome each time you take on a task or meet new people?

Here is an example of how our focus changes after doing something for the first time and how our view of life changes. Have you ever noticed in your life that when you do something for the first time, your perception of the world changes forever?

Let me give you a couple of examples. When you bought your first automobile, let's use an example of a yellow Volkswagen Beetle. I am pretty sure that by the time you drove the car off the lot, you saw other yellow Beetles driving in the same city. Maybe you did not realize nor notice before then, how many yellow Beetles were actually on the streets. Your view of the world has changed and your focus as well. You notice new things in your life without trying to, without effort.

For the ladies reading this, when you got pregnant for the first time, how many pregnant ladies did you see during your pregnancy? I bet you saw more than you did before you got pregnant.

Knowing how this works gives us a great tool to expand our mind and change our reality now, today. For example, if you start looking at property deals today, analyzing one deal per day for a whole year, by the time the year is out, you will be able to spot real estate deals wherever you travel to in the world without any effort. You will see them even when you are not looking for them. Shifting our focus and widening our perception of life is an amazing gift that we can develop within ourselves. This is true with expectations as well, when you expect your children to do well in school for example, you will find ways to make it happen. Some parents might only have to expect it, while other parents might have to help their children out, encouraging them to do better. You will start seeing all the possibilities to attract your expected results into your reality. Those parents who use the law of attraction would think something like; *"I don't know how, but my children will do well in school and I can't wait to see how the universe will deliver that into our lives."* Those parents, who know how to use the law of attraction, know their expected results will come true, and they know that the how does not matter right now, the universe will deliver it in the best possible way and at the best possible time.

HOW CAN WE USE THIS TO ATTRACT WHAT WE WANT SIMPLY BY EXPECTING RESULTS?

When you start to expect amazing things each day, something amazing will start to happen every day, it might take some time but as long as you have truly changed your expectations and you truly believe them. When we go to an event and we expect to find the perfect business partner, our mind is wide open for all the signs of that partner. What about a perfect mate for life? Write down what you expect and clearly define what your perfect partner sounds and acts like. Then become that perfect partner you described and you will be ready to spot the perfect mate you attract, by being the perfect partner yourself.

To make the expectation even more powerful, write out a detailed description about how your dream partner will make you feel, while thinking about and experiencing it like it's already happened. The stronger the energy vibration you send out the faster you attract your dream partner into your life. Expect him or her to show up in your life and your mind will be ready when that opportunity arises. You will know when that person shows up in your life. The best way to find your perfect partner is for you to become that perfect partner yourself and expect to find your match. Experience the emotions of being that perfect partner and how your perfect partner will make you feel.

WHAT ELSE HAPPENS WHEN WE START TO EXPECT RESULTS IN OUR LIFE?

We start to prepare for growth; we start to prepare ourselves for success. We start to ask questions like, when I find the business partner then what will we do to start the partnership?

When you are expecting results, like for example, when I publish this book and a lot of money starts to coming my way, what am I going to do with it, what charity am I going to support, how am I going to be able to use that money and have it work for me in the future? How can I help more people without getting overwhelmed by the success? Do I have a corporation set up to be able to use the money in the best manner possible? Do I have the right team in place to help me with taxes, will I have a good lawyer and if so, what lawyer? Who is going to be taking care of my accounting, what coaches will I have in my life once I start to build wealth, what will I invest my money in and many other questions we start asking ourselves when we expect results.

When my children start to attend school, will I be prepared to give the support needed for them to succeed like I expect? These are positive questions and by answering them we manifest the results into our lives even faster than before.

Have you heard of Robert Kiyosaki, who wrote the book *Rich Dad, Poor Dad*? Did you know that even though he was taught from an early age how to make money, when he started to really expand his company, which grew so fast, that he actually failed? Could he have prepared for success in a better manner? Absolutely and he says so himself. I saw him in an interview talking about what he should have done better. Now he talks about this experience as a learning process in his career and he recommends that people expect results and prepare for that success. His failure was growing too fast and not having enough cash-flow to sustain the growth. But he recovered very nicely, like so many that have failed, like for example, Donald Trump. He recovered well from failure as many other successful people have done. If we truly expect results in our lives we start to prepare for them as well.

HOW CAN WE TEACH OUR CHILDREN TO EXPECT SUCCESS IN LIFE?

We can encourage them in whatever venture they take on. Help them seek the information needed to succeed with their ideas and teach them that failure is not a failure, but instead just one step closer to success.

Have you seen the Disney movie *Meet the Robinsons*? That is a great movie to teach that failure is a learning step toward success. In one of the scenes in the movie, one of the characters is trying out his invention and it fails. The other characters start to cheer for the failed invention. The main character, an inventor himself, is very surprised and asks why everyone is celebrating the failed invention. The answer given is this; *"From failure we learn, from success not so much!"* What a great way to look at the attempts we make towards success. If you haven't watched that movie with your children I highly recommend it. I love entertainment that teaches us life skills and important things about life. Kung Fu Panda movie series is another example of teaching us through entertainment. In the first movie when he reads the scroll that will give him infinite power, all he sees is a reflection of himself. The power we need and can harness, lives within us from the day we are born, we just need to find it and believe it.

Failure is a part of expecting results. What is important is taking action, moving toward your expected results, even if it means failing at first. If you fail you try again, each time learning from your failure and expecting great results. This is one way how you become successful and manifest your dreams. Education through entertainment, like movies for example, is a fun and effective way to keep a variety in our teaching methods as parents.

When a person running a company says; *"I want to add a new employee"* we can tell if that person is really expecting to add a new employee to the firm with a simple observation. Has that person already set up a new desk at the office? If he has not, then he is not expecting that employee to join soon. If he was expecting to find a new employee soon, the desk should already be there or some sort of action already taken to be able to accommodate a new employee.

Expectations create a flow of positive energy that helps you to look for ways to bring your expected results into your life. When you teach your children something new and you expect certain results, but they don't learn the first time around, you will find another way to teach them the same thing with success. You are setting yourself and your children up for success, by expecting results. Expectations of results make you start thinking *"what if"* or *"when"* I succeed, how will I carry that success on to create even more success?

When the time comes that you get everything right and success shows up on your door step, usually in a greater way than you could have imagined, you have already asked yourself, can I handle it? Am I ready for all that money, am I ready for all of that abundance, am I ready for my children to excel in their field, and am I ready for the results I expect?

Are you ready for the expected outcome? Can you handle the growth? The true definition of expecting results is when you are already preparing for it so that you don't become overwhelmed when you receive the expected results. Let's take an example of a country that enters into a competition like the Eurovision song contest. If they win the competition, the country is obligated to host the competition the next year around. If the country does not have a building big enough to accommodate the competition it is very likely because they did not expect win. This does not mean that the country will not win the competition, but it definitely means they are not expecting nor ready to win it. It is OK to fail but make sure to be prepared for success; if you aren't then most likely you do not truly expect to win. When you become successful, it is very nice to be able to stay successful, and you can do that by being prepared.

Following is a ritual you can implement now, today, and let your children take part in it as well. If they don't know how to write yet, let them tell to you what to write or at least let them know what you are writing about. You are going to write a future diary with your expectations about anything you can think of.

FUTURE DIARY

The future diary is a very powerful tool that helps us to expect and manifest results in our lives. You can write about anything that has not happened yet. The more details you put in the diary the more likely it is to show up exactly as you write it. You can write about a job interview for example. A job interview you will be attending in the future. Write how you feel at the moment you go into the interview, how is the person feeling that you are meeting? What are they expecting of you and what are you expecting of them? What does the chair you are sitting on feel like? What does it feel like when they offer you the position? How are they sitting, upright or leaning towards you with enthusiasm and are they smiling? What are you going to tell them, what is your tone of voice going to sound like when you explain why you are the perfect employee for that job. The more details the better.

You can write about your child's first day at school. How the children at the school will welcome her into the new school. How many children want to become friends with your child and how fun is the school day going to be. Where will your child be sitting and how will your child feel on that day?

You can write about the next vacation you are going to take with you family. Where are you going, what are you going to see and how is the family going to feel on the vacation?

You can write about your new future office. How big is it, where is it located, what kind of furniture there, what does it feel like to go to work in your own office?

Writing things down creates a positive energy and your mind will start to look for ways to make it happen, you will start to notice things you wrote about and you will set your energy vibration into alignment with the possible new future goals and

CHAPTER 6. EXPECT RESULTS IN YOUR LIFE 71

events. The most effective way is to write on a white piece of paper using a pen with blue ink. This will make it easier for you to visualize your goals and expect them to come true. Once you start to believe, your brain and your entire body will send out the exact frequency needed to attract those results into your life.

When I started to write my future diary the results that I got were unbelievable. I had to adjust what I wrote after finding out the hard way that my words were not specific enough. I was writing about a person, let's use the alias John Johnson for privacy reasons, and I only used his first name in my diary. Here is what happened;

I dated the entry one day into the future. *"I got a phone call from John today and he told me that he likes the idea and is ready to commit and that felt great to hear. I am so happy."*

The next day I was expecting John Johnson to call me and tell me the good news. Before lunch that day John Stuart (alias as well, both have the same first name) called me and asked me how much money I needed to finish a project that had been sitting on my desk for a while, a documentary about climbing Denali, a mountain in Canada. I had forgotten about the project because there was no budget for it and I had spent over 300 hours pro-bono on it a year earlier. I told him I would be happy to finish the documentary for $15,000 and he said – OK, I am going to find the money and call you back.

Around lunch time John Williams called me to tell me that the grant I had applied for from the government had been accepted and I would be able to spend the next 9 months writing my first financial literacy course.

After lunch John Sullivan called me and asked me to participate in writing a bill for congress law changes, which their party would put up for a vote in congress if their party would be elected to sit in congress the following month, so I wrote the bill in regards to the current pension system and how the government could ensure that the amount from the pension fund would go to the family members when a loved one passed away, as this is not the case in Iceland, at least not when this book is written, currently most of the amount goes to the government.

To my surprise John Johnson had not called me that day, but instead three other persons with the same first name had and they all told me good news. I was surprised. The day after, however, John Johnson did call me to tell me that he would invest with me in the next project that I was working on at the time.

You can tell me that this was a pure coincidence, but I would just tell you that I don't believe in coincidences. The future diary is a very powerful tool, I know from experience. Make sure you put down as many details in the diary as possible, because by doing that you have greatly increased your chances of success. Remember to write about the event like it has already happened and don't forget to write about how you felt in that moment in the future. I know its may sound funny to say it like that, but you have to be able to trust the process and find out for yourself.

EXPECTATIONS THROUGH DREAM-BOARDS

Have you heard about dream-boards? It is a place where you put pictures or words you want to attract into your life, the things you expect to receive. I look at my dream-board every day and each time, I imagine what it feels like when these things start to show up in my life. Everything is about emotions, what are your emotions when you become successful? We are creating the energy flow needed to succeed by doing that. It can be a brand new bike for your children, a new house, new car, healthy lifestyle or happiness. What do you want to manifest into your life? What do you expect?

The following picture is an example of my dream-board at the time writing this. All the pictures represent something meaningful for me and I look at the dream-board before I go to bed and when I wake up. I think about what each picture represents and how I feel when I achieve it. Some of the pictures are already part of my reality now.

SUMMARY

Expecting results will increase the speed of attracting them into your life.

Expecting results will prepare you for the success, so upon reaching it you won't get overwhelmed.

Expecting to make a great first impression will set your energy vibration into alignment to actually make a great first impression and help you look for all the reasons to do just that.

Expecting results, will inspire you to prepare for the situation that you are expecting. By preparing, you have already practiced what it will feel like when the situation arrives. Making it much more likely to turn out exactly like you expect.

Writing down your expectations in a future diary will bring your vision to life and help you look for the things in life that will attract that outcome.

CHAPTER 7. RESPONSIBILITY

TAKE FULL RESPONSIBILITY FOR EVERYTHING IN YOUR LIFE

The fact that you have to take full responsibility for everything in your life might be hard to accept for many people. However when you start being fully responsible for everything in your life. That's right, everything! You start taking more control and ownership of everything, both successes and failures; and by taking ownership of your failures you also take ownership of the solutions in your life.

It was hard for me to understand and accept this fact when I first heard it. How can I be responsible for others? How is it my fault that I got hit by a bike? How is it my fault I did not get the job? How can I take responsibility for not having enough money? How can I take responsibility for my bad luck? It's not my fault!

Wrong! It is, and you might not understand it until you start taking responsibility.

I am the kind of person who needs to understand why, so I started asking people who are responsible for everything in their lives, how they do it. I asked them questions like, how is it my fault that I got hit by a bike yesterday? My friend simply said to me, it was the sum of all the decisions you made before that moment that led you to be right there and then, so you had the opportunity to be hit by the bike. It was your responsibility to look around at that moment and watch yourself. Instead you made the decision to do the opposite so you got hit by a bike. You could not have been hit by that bike at that time unless making those exact decisions that lead you to that moment.

OK, I understand that all my small decisions led me to that point but why do I need to take responsibility for being hit by a bike someone else was riding? Because that is the only thing you can take responsibility for, your life and everything that is your perception of reality.

I was starting to get it, but I was not convinced at the time. Have you ever heard about people that are so lucky, they are always in the right place at the right time to find amazing deals and make a lot of money? I have.

Some would call it luck, but people who live by the creed of taking responsibility for their lives, know that it's actually not luck. It is the outcome of preparation, decisions, hard work and taking responsibility, that lead them to the point of being in the right place at the right time, having the opportunity to recognize the amazing deal being presented to them. The more they practice this, the more they find themselves being at the right place at the right time and it only gets better and better. We don´t say; *"Wow, you are lucky!"*, to a person that has managed to find 30 amazing deals during the period of one year.

No, we know that person knows something we don't. That person has spent time and money on education and preparation to be able to find those deals.

The harder I practice, the luckier I get.

The more I practice, the luckier I get.

The more they put out, the more luck they have.

The harder he works, the luckier he gets.

The more you know the more luck you have.

Have you ever read any of these quotes before? Do they make sense to you? Do you think that you might be considered lucky after spending 10 years practicing your skills in finding property deals all over the world? Do you think after spending those 10 years of practicing those skills, that you would consider yourself lucky? What about sports, those who have 20 years of experience in golf, are they luckier than beginners?

LEAD BY EXAMPLE FOR YOUR CHILDREN AND TAKE RESPONSIBILITY FOR EVERYTHING IN YOUR LIFE

Teach your children to take full responsibility and tell them that their current results are the sum of everything they do and think. If they feel like a victim at school it is your responsibility to encourage them to be responsible for their current situation, by teaching them how to change their mindset; how to make better decisions and so forth. By teaching them, you are taking responsibility for the situation.

I was bullied at school when I was very young and I told my father about it. He told me stories about how he always stood up for others at school, because he was very strong when he was young. I reacted to his stories by starting practicing judo, and three years later I stood up to the biggest bully on campus, taking him down, without hurting him a lot, just enough so that I was never bullied again. Many years later, my former bully became my friend. I am not saying violence is the answer, but this story illustrates how I took responsibility and solved my situation at the time, and how my dad took responsibility encouraging me to change my mindset and make better decisions. Our children are in our reality which means we have to take responsibility for them as well.

Hopefully you are starting to grasp the idea of taking responsibility for your life, like I did when it was explained to me at first. The questions now are; can we take responsibility for more than just ourselves, for others as well? Can we take total responsibility? *"Yes, we can."* You might agree that we as parents have to take responsibility for our children, and to do so we need to realize that they are just small people, not children. The sooner we realize that the sooner we can start treating and teaching them appropriately. Just by changing your perception of your child you can change the way you teach your child essential life skills.

When I was in high school I was placed in a class that was awful. The children were loud and did not show the teacher any respect. I often saw my classmates being thrown out of the classroom, I even saw one of my classmates threaten the teacher when she was about to throw him out. He told her he'd be waiting for her after the class and that he would beat her up. I went to my dad and told him I did not like my class, they were so bad; I could not learn anything even if I wanted to. He told me that I should take responsibility for the classroom. I did not understand him and said; *"how can I do that? I am only an average student and I can't influence the whole classroom."* He told me to go to school the next day and take responsibility and expect the class to start behaving better. Hesitantly I followed his advice. The next day I sat in class only thinking about this, I sat quietly and just watched my classmates the whole day. Believe it or not, I never saw anyone get thrown out of the classroom again. The class did not become the best class in school but they did improve and I mean really improve. Was that a coincidence? I believe not.

Many of the stories I share in the book to illustrate a point, did not make sense to me until later in life. I did what my father told me and taught me without thinking about the HOW or WHAT. I just did it because I believed at the time that my father knew everything. I looked up to him and I still do, but today I also know that he has flaws that I adapted early on and had have been getting in the way of my success. Today I carefully select new methods I adapt, correct old bad habits and hang on to the good habits I adapted early on from my father.

Let's look at a story that Joe Vitale shared in one of his books I read. He shared a story about a man who takes total responsibility. He heard about a therapist in Hawaii who cured a complete ward of criminally insane patients. That, by itself, is outstanding, but what was truly amazing to me is that the therapist did so, without seeing any of the patients during his 4 years at the ward. Instead, he took total responsibility for their illness since they were now a part of his reality. The healing method that the therapist, Dr. Ihaleakala Hew Len, used is called ho'oponopono. At the time he decided to take on this task, the ward was known for violence, unhappy staff members and the turnover of psychologists was very high.

Dr. Len worked at the ward for four years before they shut it down, reason being that all the patients were cured and released. Dr. Len agreed to have his office at the ward, but instead of working on the patients, he only worked on himself. After only a few months, the patients started to heal and the staff started to feel better. What was he doing to himself that was causing others to heal?

Dr. Len believes that everyone has to take total responsibility for their lives, and everything within their reality simply because it is part of them.

If you want to improve anything in your life, there is only one place you have to look, inside of you. We are born with such powers that it often takes us many years before we even start to understand how powerful we really are, and some people will never know. Dr. Len would read the patients files in his office and take full responsibility for their illness repeating these words;

I love you

Please forgive me

I am sorry

Thank you

I use this method myself. Although not to the same extent as Dr. Len did for 4 years straight. I use it today when I feel frustration towards people who I do not want to lose contact with but at the same time know they do not influence my life in a positive way on my journey of personal growth. I use this method if I get frustrated towards anyone. I catch myself right away and ask myself why I am feeling this way and why my emotions are changed because of something that someone else said or did. I know I am not supposed to let other people influence me in a negative way and I know that I need to stay at a high frequency level if I am going to change the world. As soon as I realize that, I repeat the words until I feel myself back on track.

One of the key elements to success is to start associating yourself with people who are smarter than you, richer than you, people that have done more than you and parents who you consider role models in their parenting. By surrounding yourself with people you look up to or who inspire you, you gain the most experience and wisdom. What about the people who you cannot stop seeing, your family, your siblings or spouse? They might be holding you back yet you are unable to simply fire them from your life. If possible you should associate less with them, and use the self healing ho'oponopono method, which will do wonders for you in that situation. I personally use this method almost daily in my life. I use it when I feel any resistance to my goals, any frustration or any bad feeling towards the people who I am around and I am not willing to get rid off. It works best for me to say things out loud, so I go to an empty room or simply say it in the car while driving.

I love you

Please forgive me

I am sorry

Thank you

I will repeat this until I feel that I have shifted my energy vibration or the bad feeling has left my body. I have also noticed a change in the people who I associate with and I know I have something to do with it, because I take more and more responsibility for my life, total responsibility. I know this is a method I will work with, throughout my life and like anything else we do; we do not become masters of anything overnight.

YOUR EGO CAN DESTROY YOUR ABILITY TO TAKE RESPONSIBILITY

I watched a presentation by Jocko Willink and Leif Babin, former US Navy Seals officers, explaining how your ego can destroy your ability to take responsibility for your life. In this short presentation they explain that the Navy Seals are very well trained and mentally tough. They are very driven by their ego and they compete in everything they do. Because they are driven by ego, their ego grows each time they reach a new goal or a new milestone. When their ego becomes too big for their own good, the blaming game starts. They are so well trained that it cannot be their fault when they fail, or so they think. They cannot accept criticism and they think they know best. They blame their crew members, their team and even their superiors. Even the super well trained and talented Navy Seals try to avoid the responsibility they should be embracing. We see that the blaming game is not just applicable to regular people but people from all walks of life.

Being humble is a virtue. Being able to take ownership of your failure is key, both in creating success and for further development. By taking ownership of failure you take ownership of solutions as well. I really liked the way the two former US Navy Seals put it;

"If we get caught off guard by our enemies, who are we going to blame? We can't, it is our fault, we were not ready!"

I love this quote as well;

"You cannot surround yourself with negative people and expect to live a positive life."

Unknown

HOW CAN WE HELP OUR CHILDREN TO TAKE RESPONSIBILITY FOR THEIR LIVES?

This is my opinion and what I teach my children if I catch them lying to me or blaming others for something they did. I start by, working with them, asking them questions, until they admit what they did or admit that it was their responsibility. At this stage I make sure to tell them that I am not going to punish them for whatever it was, because I want them to be able to talk to me about anything. I make sure to explain to them that I want them to be honest with me and to be able to take responsibility for their actions. The next step I take is to discuss how we can fix what's happened. Did they break something? How can we fix it, if we can't fix it, then how much is it going to cost to replace it and how can we create the money needed to mend it? Did they do something to someone else? Again, how do we fix that, can we go and tell that person we are sorry? Can we do more than that, if so, what and how? Their punishment is helping them realize how their actions reflect on themselves as human beings and that they need to take responsibility for their actions.

Often these are very simple tasks to overcome and learn from, but sometimes it takes a lot of time and effort to work on mending the situation. Both instances are totally worth it.

SUMMARY

Take total responsibility for your reality and your failures by which you take ownership of the solutions as well.

Take responsibility for all the people within your reality, if you can't, fire them from your life. Some will automatically distance themselves as you grow more successful.

Repeating these phrases; please forgive me, I am sorry, I love you and thank you, shift yourself back into alignment and help you take responsibility for everything in your reality.

When you start taking responsibility for everything in your life you realize that you are the creator of your reality and you can shape it however you want.

When you start taking responsibility you will see how much you truly affect your environment.

CHAPTER 8. LAW OF ATTRACTION

The basics of the law of attraction is that **you will attract into your life whatever you focus on and think about most of the time with the greatest emotion behind it**. Focusing on your goals with positive emotions, and focusing on positive things attracts more positive outcomes into your life. Concentrating on sickness and negativity will attract more negativity and sickness into your life. If your energy is spent on worrying about bills, that is exactly what you will attract into your life, more bills! The foundation to making the law of attraction work, is to feel good today. How can you feel a little bit better now before you start to think about your goals as if you have already achieved them? The better you feel when thinking about your goals, the more powerful your energy vibration becomes and the faster the universe will deliver the results to you.

We live in the state of creation, every minute of your lives. You are always creating the results you attract into your life based on your thoughts, emotions and actions. The law of attraction is a law, meaning that it is always at work just like the law of gravity. The more you think about abundance and happiness the more positive energy you send out to the universe. The more you think about your dreams and goals with a great feeling behind the thought, the more power is being applied through the law of attraction. The universe will respond to your energy vibration with enthusiasm regardless of what state of vibration you are in. If you are in a bad state of vibration and sending out bad energy, the universe gets enthusiastic about that energy and helps you receive more of that same energy.

One step to start attracting what you want into your life is to start responding consciously to situations instead of reacting subconsciously to them. By responding consciously you can focus your energy in a positive way towards the situation you find yourself in. Do you want to attract more happiness and love into your life? Then you need to tune into that frequency and you will start attracting more of the frequency right away. By choosing to start responding consciously to situations in your life you start to attract new and more positive results. If you choose to keep on doing what you have always been doing, you will keep getting the same results you have been getting up until now.

"The definition of insanity is to do the same thing over and over again and expect different results."

Albert Einstein.

BE OBSESSED OR BE AVERAGE

Obsession is one of your greatest gifts in life. Some might think that being obsessed is bad, but looking at how the law of attraction works, obsession is great. The more you think about what you are obsessed about, the faster you attract more of the same into your life. If you agree with Grant Cardone that obsession is positive, then you can start to notice the things that you are obsessed about right now and channel them in the right direction. I am not saying you need to become successful or rich, I am saying if you become obsessed you can! Are you obsessed with TV? Are you obsessed with drinking alcohol? Are you obsessed to be a great parent? Grant Cardone shared in his book *BE OBSESSED OR BE AVERAGE*, that the drug habits he used to have were due to not allowing himself to become obsessed with his true passions. Yes, he has many passions and many purposes, and he pursues them all with an unapologetic obsession. You can have many obsessions as well, but are you allowing yourself to follow them and let go of your delusion that obsession is bad? Are you doing something today that has become an obsession and you know it's not serving your purpose at all? I am pretty sure there are some things in your life right now that you obsessed about. Can you imagine what will happen if you become obsessed about something that serves your purpose? Do you notice what all the great people in the world have in common? People who have changed the world in some way, are all obsessed! What's truly stopping you from letting yourself become obsessed with your success story? Is it your family? Maybe your friends and co-workers? Are you living your life for someone else today? When will you be ready to unleash the power that resides within you right now and become obsessed about being great at something? If you want to change then something has to change.

When I was 15 years old, my biggest dream was to go and play basketball in the US. I had just started playing basketball and I was considered very promising, but not good enough yet. All I could think about was to go to America. At 16, in 1993, I got a friend of mine who has ties to the US to help me make a basketball reel of me doing drills on the basketball court, supervised and directed by him. He was experienced in helping basketball players get into US colleges. We sent the tape to a few high schools, and I got selected to go to a high school in Pennsylvania where a very nice family decided to host me. My dream was about to become real. I bought the plane ticket, but 2 weeks before my departure, the family contacted me and said they were so sorry but due to family issues, they could no longer accommodate me.

I was shocked and sad. But I kept on thinking about playing in the US, that was all I wanted. Each time I thought about it I felt great, like it had already happened. Every time I thought about playing basketball in the US, I got butterflies in my stomach. At that time I did not know anything about the law of attraction, but that does not matter, because I, as all of us, use the law each day by the selection of thoughts and by how much emotion is put behind each thought. With my dream on hold, I played basketball in Iceland and did really well, started to become a decent player and won several gold medals with my team there.

I started to look at junior colleges trying to find a way to go to America and play basketball, I was obsessed with my dream. In the spring of 1997 I went with the junior national team to play in Sweden in an international basketball tournament. I was scouted by a coach from Norway who wanted me to come and play with his team that fall. He was a former US college basketball coach and told me he would help me get to the US if I would come and play with his team. I was very excited. I took a contract home with me from the coach, which I, and my parents as witnesses, signed.

However, sometimes the law of attraction works in a strange way, and here is an example of how;

In July 1997 I was ready to send the contract to Norway, buy a ticket and move there, when I got a phone call from my friend who tried to help me in 1993 with the basketball reel. He told me that a coach he knew in the US wanted two players from Iceland to come and join his team and get a full scholarship at the university. Why was he willing to offer a full scholarships to players he had not even seen in person?

In the beginning of the summer 1997 the former basketball coach at Campbellsville University had a heart attack and died. Travis Ford, became the new head coach at the university, but it was so late in the summer that he had few options to recruit players. He decided to call a friend of his in Iceland, my friend as well, and ask him for help. He still had two full scholarships to give out but having gotten the coaching position so late in the summer forced him to rely on the word of our mutual friend. I contacted the coach in Norway telling him it was my dream to play in the US and I was going for it. He understood that and congratulated me.

I flew to the states in August 1997 and experienced my dream. I was living my dream. I experienced for the first time what great coaches can do for you, they take you to the next level you would not reach on your own. The coaches at the university were top notch and because I have great work ethics, I was in the best shape of my life. I am so grateful today for my 5 years in Kentucky, both for the highs and lows. I graduated from Campbellsville University, with a bachelor's degree in business administration, in 2002. This is how the law of attraction works in a nutshell, you can never know how exactly you attract things into your life. However if you think about your goals most of the time, with a great feeling and positive emotions, the universe will deliver exactly that to you, often in the most unexpected way, exactly at the right time.

WE ARE ENERGY LIKE EVERYTHING ELSE IN THE WORLD

We know that there is something in this universe that is part of everything and flows through everything. What is this power that keeps everything in working order? If we ask a scientist and a theologian to explain to us what is the power that keeps everything in the universe in working order, they will gives us two different answers. The scientist will tell us that this power is energy. That energy is everywhere and keeps the world in working order, the energy just is, it can neither be created nor destroyed. The theologian, however, will tell us that this power is called God. God is everywhere and keeps everything is working order, God can neither be created nor destroyed, he just is. Even though I was born into Christianity, I like to call this power The Source, for the simple reason that I can then refer to it without conflict of religions. In my experience many people are not open to new views or discussions when it comes to religions.

At one of Bob Proctor's events he refers to this analogy and says that science and theology will eventually find out that they are studying the same power, the only difference is that scientists are studying the energy that surrounds us while theologians which are studying the energy within us. Being a person fond of facts and loving science, I will be using the word "energy" in this book.

Everything in this world is energy in a different vibrational state of frequency. You are a bundle of intelligent energy walking around in a form of a body. Energy can neither be created nor destroyed; we can only change the vibrational state. Energy will always pull or push, that is why you are a magnet both, receiving and giving energy. When your energy vibration is at a certain frequency you attract the same frequency just like a radio, but when you change to a different frequency, that new frequency is being attracted to you. When you are in a positive state of mind you attract positive things into your life and push negative things out. When you are in a negative state of mind and your energy vibration is at a low frequency you attract more negative energy and push away positive energy.

Today you are the result of what you have felt, thought and done in the past. You are the result of your own creation, but that does not reflect who you will become from now on. You can decide to change your energy today and start attracting both positive energy and positive results into your life. You can start attracting whatever you desire, you are the creator.

"You are the results of what you have thought."

Buddha

MOST OF US HAVE NO IDEA HOW POWERFUL WE REALLY ARE.

Your thoughts are measurable with the use of modern technology. Your thoughts are real things, not just something intangible.

"Thought is action in rehearsal."

Sigmund Freud

Your thoughts are energy. Your thoughts are so powerful that they create a physical reaction in you and your environment. We can use science to take a polygraph test and see if you are lying for example. Every single cell in your body is affected by your thoughts.

Negative thoughts create a negative environment in your body. They can create tension and lead to an acidic state. An acidic state in the body is the ideal environment for diseases to thrive in, like cancer for example. Positive thoughts however create a positive environment in your body, increasing the release of endorphins and relaxing your body. Positive thoughts are 10 to 100 times more powerful than negative thoughts. It is therefore important for us to shift our negative mindset as soon as we realize it and focus on something positive, you can even use the anchoring technique, from chapter 5, to shift your energy vibration into a higher frequency. We influence our children by our thoughts and it's important to try and keep most of them positive. We can teach our children to reverse any negativity, and turn it into a positive thought process.

NEGATIVE THOUGHTS SLOW YOU DOWN ON YOUR JOURNEY TO SUCCESS

Imagine that you are pulling a wagon up a hill, and on top of that hill is your success. When you think positive thoughts you gain strength and start to pull the wagon uphill. Every time you start thinking negatively, your power weakens and you stop pulling because the road to success is uphill, you might even slide backward a bit. On your journey to the top of the hill you have all the people you surround yourself with on that wagon. The positive people sit on the side of the wagon, with their legs touching the ground, helping you push the wagon uphill. However the negative people, or the free loaders, go all the way up on top the wagon, sitting comfortably making the wagon that much heavier to pull up the hill. The more positive thoughts you have the more positive energy you send out and more positive energy you receive. Therefore more positive people start to come and sit on your wagon, into your life, helping you to push the wagon uphill.

Think about what type of people you want to have on your wagon, the type who make it heavier or the type that help you by pushing and help you succeed with positivity. The positive people you surround yourself with, boost your confidence and boost your positive thinking even more.

Your conscious mind is powerful but limited by the selection of your thoughts. On the other hand your subconscious mind has no known limits, only the limits you have placed on it yourself, with your beliefs. Your subconscious mind is your connection to The Source, the energy that keeps everything in the universe in working order.

MEDITATION IS ONE OF THE TECHNIQUES WE CAN USE TO TAP INTO THE POWER OF THE SUBCONSCIOUS MIND

Meditation is about relaxing your body and mind and diving into the pool of infinite wisdom and creativity. There are many ways to meditate. I use a technique that was introduced to the world by Maharishi Mahesh Yogi. The technique is called Transcendental Meditation or often referred to as TM. It is one of many meditation techniques available. To explain how meditation works we can say that your conscious mind is the top layer of thought and when you slow it down with meditation, you calm the conscious mind. Imagine a water puddle and each time you are using your conscious mind you stir dirt in the water puddle, making it impossible to see the bottom. Meditation keeps the water puddle still allowing the dirt to settle down and you start to see further down in it. Imagine that the bottom of the puddle is where you can access your subconscious mind and infinite wisdom and each time you calm the water, you are able to see, and go, a little bit further down taking more and more wisdom back with you to the top again.

This is a simple way for you to explain to your children how meditation works. Of course it is a simple metaphor of what is really happening while meditating. When a person reaches enlightenment, that person starts to be able to work and live in their normal state with a clear water puddle, working as one with the energy that resides within us all, The Source. There are no limits. Once a person is enlightened he/she will always make the right decision according to all the laws of nature.

EVERYTHING WE DO INFLUENCES THE STATE WE LIVE IN

What you watch on TV, what you read, what you focus on, what you talk about, and what you do, has a direct effect on your state of mind. A big part of being a parent is teaching your children that whatever they watch has a direct effect on their state of being. The more they watch positive movies, the more positive they will become, the more positive books they read, the more positively they think, and the more positive things you talk about with your children, the more positive you and your children become.

SHOWING AND GIVING YOUR CHILDREN LOVE IS VERY IMPORTANT

When we live in the state of love we are close to the highest emotional frequency state we can reach. It is one of the easiest ways to increase the positive energy vibration in you and your children, when you are in the state of love. There has been a lot of research done on love. Some of the researches I have read about love, were conducted on orphans.

In the 1940's people began to question why the death rate of infants at orphanages was so high. It was thought to be due to contagious diseases. An Austrian psychoanalyst and physician, Rene Spitz, thought differently. He believed that the orphans were dying because of lack of love. To test his theory he monitored two groups of infants, a group of orphans in an orphanage, which was kept as sterile as possible to prevent diseases, and a group of infants being raised by their own incarcerated mothers in prison. If the theory of infants dying from diseases was true, then the children in the orphanage should have done better than the children in the prison, but this was not the case. 37% of the infants in the orphanage died during the study but all the infants in the prison lived. The infants in the prison grew faster, and became larger, and in fact, they did better in every way that Spitz could measure.

From this study it was clear that the lack of love was what had these devastating results of infant deaths in orphanages. Loving your children is like watering a plant, you have to show it on a regular basis and your children need to feel it. Don't be afraid to show it as often as possible.

I was raised in a home where my mother would show me love but my father did not, or at least in a very particular way. He was raised in a hostile environment where punishments were frequent and he endured a lot of adversity and cruelty. He was, and still is, a very closed introvert person who has trouble showing affection, this influenced me in a big way. My father taught me so much about life and he was good to me. Even though I was sometimes punished with physical punishments like spankings, I could see the importance of it and appreciated his efforts in every way. I do not believe in physical punishment today. I show my children and tell them that I love them, but I did not at first. I had to consciously decide that. I said to myself that is who I have to become to be a good parent. Love yourself and your children and find yourself in a state of positive energy vibration, where everything is possible. Love life, love living. Love, cannot only bring your state of being to a higher energy frequency, but also everyone else around you.

HOW HIGH DOES LOVE SCORE COMPARED TO OTHER ENERGY STATES OF BEING?

We will use a scale from the book Power vs. Force by David R. Hawkins to illustrate how high love scores compared to other states of being. The table is based on his research and the scores range from from 20 to 1000.

Level	Log	Emotion	Life View
Enlightenment	700-1000	Ineffable	Is
Peace	600	Bliss	Perfect
Joy	540	Serenity	Complete
Love	500	Reverence	Benign
Reason	400	Understanding	Meaningful
Acceptance	350	Forgiveness	Harmonious
Willingness	310	Optimism	Hopeful
Neutrality	250	Trust	Satisfactory
Courage	200	Affirmation	Feasible
Pride	175	Scorn	Demanding
Anger	150	Hate	Antagonistic
Desire	125	Craving	Disappointing
Fear	100	Anxiety	Frightening
Grief	75	Regret	Tragic
Apathy	50	Despair	Hopeless
Guilt	30	Blame	Evil
Shame	20	Humiliation	Miserable

Christie Marie Sheldon referenced his studies at an event where she talked about changing your frequency to change your reality.

Scoring 20 is the lowest level of shame, where you feel like you are not enough, not worthy.

Apathy or level 50 is the level where many homeless people are at; it represents the state of not caring anymore or giving up.

Fear is at the level of 100. An example of fear is questioning, what if I make too much money and other people want to take it all away from me.

Desire at the level of 125 is to desire or crave something to uplift yourself, you are not enough, but with this "something" you will be.

Level 150 is anger and that is the first stage in this scale that starts to move energy around you, not necessarily good, but at least it is starting to move.

Courage is at the level of 200 which is considered to be right around the average for the human race.

Acceptance at level 350 is when you accept responsibility for a bigger part of your life, your reality.

Reasoning at level 400 is where Albert Einstein was measured at, he scored 495 on this scale.

> Level 500 is the level of love and living in the state of love enables you to positively impact up to 750.000 people.
>
> Joy scores 540 on the scale, at this stage you start to be able to heal what is needed in your life, so start playing and having fun.
>
> When a person is at peace, or at level 600, that person can positively impact up to 10 million people.
>
> Finally a person who is at level 700, or enlightenment, can positively impact up to 70 million people.

Your state of emotions is often the result of your state of mind. It is possible for you to decide to change your state of mind to reach a higher frequency of emotions. Emotions are triggered by your beliefs and you can reprogram your beliefs.

> *"Everything you see happening is the consequence of that which you are."*
>
> David R. Hawkins

One experiment, that was conducted to prove how we impact people, was conducted by the Maharishi Foundation and the results of that study is now called the Maharishi Effect. They had 7,000 meditative participants and placed them in different cities, measuring various effects on the city before, after, and during the meditation. The results were astounding, reducing crime rate down by 16% at average for example. The Maharishi Effect is defined as "one percent of the population practicing the

Transcendental Meditation Program in any city reduces the crime rate, accident rate, and sickness rate" and "establishes a new formula for the creation of an ideal society, free from crime and problems, and with this, Maharishi envisions the dawn of a new age for mankind, the Age of Enlightenment." I encourage you to look up the study if you want to read more about the positive impact we can have on our environment.

If you have regrets or are holding on to resentment toward anyone, it is time for you to let it go. These feelings are only holding you back from the growth you should be experiencing right now.

"Not forgiving someone is like drinking poison and expecting the other person to die."

Unknown

You attract what you focus on, that is the law of attraction. Richard Branson shared, that one of the biggest reasons he is so successful is that he forgives people who do him wrong and he always gives people a second chance. It is as important as to forgive yourself. In case you haven't, do that right now, forgive yourself for anything you are holding on to from your past, release yourself, to be able to grow.

"If you haven't forgiven yourself something, how can you forgive others?"

Dolores Huerta

When you decide to live in abundance and happiness the universe responds to that. Some might think something like this; *"I don't want to be sad."* However, **the universe, the power around us, does not understand the statement *"don't"*,** so it will respond to that thought as it being; *"I want to be sad."* If you are really sad and thinking about not being sad, the universe, with enthusiasm, will respond with the same energy as yours.

What do you think about, when someone tells you, **not** to think about an elephant? What do you need to do, to make the universe respond to your desired state of mind? You need to think about the opposite, you need to change that into a positive statement of desire. Example; *"I want to be happy."* It sounds simple when you know that. To make the statement even more positive, we change "want" to "will", *"I will be happy"* or *"I am happy."* Many people are stuck, because they keep on asking for change, with statements that include "don't" and "not". The same applies, when you are parenting your children, notice if they use negative words to describe their desires; *"Daddy I don't want to be picked on anymore at school."* If they are at the age of understanding, explain to them why they need to change this statement. If you have younger children, simply start by asking them what they want instead, try and have them say it themselves, but if it is not making sense, help them and tell to them to say for example; *"Daddy I am going to get more compliments at school."* After which you can start talking about ways you can attract that into their lives. You have now taken their focus off the negativity, thinking about positive things and possible solutions to achieve that goal.

I had to change a lot of beliefs I was raised up with, to be able to use the law of attraction like it should be used.

When I was 4 years old I told my father that I wanted to become a bank manager. He understood why I said it and told me that the bank manager does not own the money in the bank. I then withdrew my wish of becoming a bank manager. I was 4 years old when I realized that we had little money, we were poor. My father recently told me, that at one point the household income was 10,000 ISK after tax, at the same time as the interest on their bank loan was 12,000 ISK per month, and that was only the interest. That's what you call a messed up situation! Of course I did not know any numbers then but I knew we did not have any money. When I was approximately 5 years old I asked my father to help me write a letter, although I knew the letters, I didn't yet know how to write. He said OK. I wanted him to help me write a letter to my grandparents, who had some wealth at the time, and I asked him to help me write; *"Please send some money, we are so poor."*, by saying each letter so I could write it myself. He talked with me about how we should take care of this ourselves and that we should not be asking for help. The letter ended up something like this; *"Hi grandma and grandpa, how are you doing? We are great. Sincerely, Huni."*

The two beliefs that I needed to change to be able to use the law of attraction, were my beliefs of having to do everything myself and that it was OK to be poor. I started at a young age to earn my own money but with no guidance or role model on how to earn, manage or invest money. I failed over and over again, throughout my life. If I came across any money, it would disappear out of my life as fast as it had arrived. Throughout my schooling I did not learn how to earn and manage money. Even with a Master's degree in Business, I have had to change my beliefs from my past, my conditioning from my parents, in order to be able to grow and start to attract wealth and success. I used the law of attraction for the first 35 years of my life to attract bills and not to trust anyone to help me on my journey.

TAKING ACTION USING THE LAW OF ATTRACTION

Know what you don't want and change it into a desirable goal. Identify what you do want so you can start focusing on it in a positive way, attracting what you truly want into your life. When you go into a restaurant, do you start by listing, to the waiter, all the things you don't want? No, you only ask for what you want. You should be asking for the things you want in life and not concentrating on the things you don't want. Go ahead and place your order for your desired life and remember to do so while feeling great, like it has already happened.

Declare your intentions, turn complaints into statements of positive objectives. Get rid of negative beliefs within you and manifest NOW by experiencing what it feels like when you have achieved it.

Let go of the need for something, while taking action. Rather than asking for something with a feeling of need, do it with desire, like when being pulled underwater, desiring air into your lungs. When you want something as bad as you want to breathe, the law of attraction will work fast and in an amazing way.

CHANGING YOUR ENVIRONMENT

Choose to stay out of negativity. Turn off the media, they are experts at feeding you negativity, so select carefully what you watch and listen to. Feed your mind with positive material. Choose positive things to watch, read and listen to.

Get support! 3-6 people to hold you accountable for your transformation, a mastermind group of people who are growing and helping one another to do the same.

Get a coach. Having someone outside your own limiting beliefs helps you expand your beliefs and go beyond what you could do on your own.

Find a friend to share your transformation with, and support each other.

WEALTH MINDSET AND TAKING ACTION TOWARDS YOUR FINANCIAL GOALS

Start giving right now and you shall start receiving.

Eliminate your block, your limited belief about money, that for example, money is evil, money is not good for you, or money just doesn't like you. If your block is thinking that money is bad for you, find the positive benefits of that belief. Why do you think that? Is it to protect you from getting hurt? What's the positive benefit from that belief? Staying safe, being normal.

The statement would then sound like this; *"The belief that money is bad for me causes me to feel safe and not judged."* If this is your reasoning, does it make sense? I believe the total opposite. When you start manifesting money into your life with the law of attraction, you can start feeling safe and not judged. Financial security equals safety. This is one way of looking at the problem and finding the positive reasoning behind your beliefs and being able to turn that belief into the opposite. Money is good for me. I love money. I deserve money. Money loves me.

Take action. Find a cause to believe in and get involved.

Get support from, for example, friends, coaches, or a mastermind group. Be grateful. Follow your enthusiasm. Take responsibility for everything in your life.

WHAT IS YOUR TRUE PURPOSE IN LIFE?

This easy exercise will help you define what your true purpose is, it will also help you in creating your action plan on how you will share your true mission with the world.

> On a piece of paper list down, in numeric order, the things you like to do, want to do, and that give you pleasure in life. Don't think about how to do it or what it costs. You might go to 40 things or even more than a 100 before you start to seeing a pattern in your list. You can do the same thing with your children, listing down what they like to do and what makes them feel good. It might be a little early in life for them to identify their life

purpose, but it might be the right time to find it, depending on the age of your children and maturity.

This simple exercise will help you to understand how your children look at life and what they truly want to spend time doing. When you see the patterns emerging from their list, you can help your children to further pursue their passions and interests. You can contribute to their well-being and happiness. The same applies to you. Remember to list things you would like to do regardless of the cost. Don't limit your list; this list has nothing to do with what you can afford or what you have time to do today. As the list grows you are likely to see a pattern shaping, similar sentences occurring, use these to see if you can identify your true life purpose.

My true purpose is to empower parents to teach their children life skills from an early age to enable the children to grow up without limiting themselves and having the chance to become the best generation yet on this planet.

CREATE A BUCKET LIST

List all the things you want to accomplish in life, it could be anywhere from 50-150 things, even more. Look at the list regularly and remember to tick off the completed goals. This is a list that will help you monitor and manifest your dreams throughout your life. You don't need any explanations on how you will achieve these goals. You will think about the how, when it comes to executing the next goal on the list, or even better, when you get good at using the law of attraction you can simply look forward to see how the Universe will reveal the HOW to you, knowing that the bucket list items will be accomplished. Once you decide what the next goal to achieve is, you will either think about HOW or watch how the universe will deliver the HOW to you, one goal at a time.

Help you children to make their own initial list and they can gradually add new things to the list as they learn more about life. You can always add to your list as well. Include both small and big goals on your list, every goal you can possibly think of wanting to achieve in life. The law of attraction will play a big role in manifesting these goals.

Many people find it difficult to start believing in the transformation. It is OK not to believe in the beginning. If you follow the rituals, change your mindset, set goals, clear blocks, and start striving towards your goals, you will start believing once see the changes in your life, or when people start to compliment you on the changes they notice.

Many of the most successful people in the world started writing down goals without believing in them at first, but they did not give up, and at a certain point in time they started believing and at which point their success really took off.

If you read a lie on a piece of paper every day you will eventually start believing that lie, and it can become your truth. This is just a metaphor of course, because the goals are not lies, even though they might seem like it in the beginning. Just take the first step and keep on taking one step at a time and you will attract the results into your life and your children's lives. A person that has not heard about the law of gravity for example, might be skeptical towards it, the same might be said about the law of attraction. Make no mistake about it though, it is a law and the law of attraction works whether you believe in it or not.

Be grateful right now for everything. Before you go to sleep each night look back at the day that past and be grateful for the events of that day remembering to acknowledge the people who help you on the way.

SUMMARY

Law of attraction will attract anything you focus on with positive energy and positive emotions into your life.

What you focus on and think about, grows.

We impact our environment massively, positively or negatively.

Keep thinking about your goals, about WHY and WHEN and you will attract the results and see how the universe will bring the HOW into your life.

If you are attracting bad results right now, and you want to change them into good results, you might need to change your beliefs first.

Start giving to start receiving.

Forgive yourself first, then everyone else. Let go of the negativity in your life regardless of the magnitude. Release the ropes holding you down so you can start to soar towards your goals.

The law of attraction does not always attract the results into your life like you expect. It might be a surprise to you when you see how and when they show up.

CHAPTER 9. ALIGNMENT AND VIBRATION

Are you in alignment? Have you heard this question before? Do you know if you are in alignment?

You might realize that to be able to answer this question, you actually need to be more specific. When you ask yourself the question if you are in alignment, you need to ask in alignment with what subject. This could be your spouse for example, are you two in alignment? You and your children, are you aligned? Are you aligned with your goals?

How do you know when you are in alignment? It's pretty simple, if everything falls into place, everything seems easy and everything feels awesome, you are most likely in alignment. Some people would say that it was meant to be, and that is almost the same thing as to be in alignment.

The next question is; *"how is your vibration?"* What are we asking, when we ask about your vibration? A shift in your vibration of energy can snap you into alignment. It can also trigger you out of alignment.

"You must bring yourself into alignment with what you are asking for. That's what joy is, that's what appreciation is, that's what the feeling of passion is. But when you are feeling despair, or fear, or anger, those are strong indicators that you are not right now in alignment with what you are asking for."

Esther Hicks

Let's start by going into the basics and looking at what vibration really means. When we try to explain to a young child what God, the source, or the creator is, we could explain it like this for example;

> *"In the beginning there was only energy and the energy was then later transformed into another state of vibration."*

Everything known to us today as material or matter, is a form of energy in different states of vibration. Science has provided us with proof that energy can neither be destroyed nor created, but merely transformed into another form of energy, a process also known as changing the vibrational state of that energy. Let's take a glass of water as an example. The water is energy at a certain level of vibration. If we take heat and apply it to the glass we can transform the water into steam. This is another vibratory state of the energy that used to be in the form of water. If we continue to apply heat to the steam it will eventually turn into gas and blend with the atmosphere, eventually turn into clouds and finally back to water in the form of rain. If we apply frost to the water, we also change the vibrational state of the water into ice. This is of course a simplified explanation of energy and then the change in its vibratory state, but true nevertheless.

THE POWER OF WORDS

CHAPTER 9. ALIGNMENT AND VIBRATION

Scientists have been fascinated by water for a long time. We know that water contains great power, but yet we know so little about it today. We do know a few things about water though and we are learning more each year. We are always seeking new ways to harness the energy from water. We can also use water to detect other things, let's look at an example.

The late Dr. Masaru Emoto got the idea in 1994 to start an experiment on water and see if he could measure the effects of the energy vibration humans send out on the water. He would say something to the water, play music or even offer a prayer, and after that he would freeze it. The last phase of the experiment was to take the frozen water, slice it, take a picture of it with a microscope and see if there was any difference in the water crystals when he used positive words versus when he would use negative words. His experiment proved without a doubt that we can see the effects on water when we shift our energy vibration. Every time we think or say something we are sending a vibration out to the universe, and our vibrational state affects our environment. The reason for some words affecting us with negative vibration and some with positive vibration is our social conditioned programming since we were born. A certain word will trigger a certain energy vibration because we connect this word to a positive or negative experience. To read more about the experiments and see the water crystal pictures go to this site; www.masaru-emoto.net

It is incredible to see how much difference it makes on the water crystals when we use words like; *"compassion"*, *"thank you"*, *"wisdom"*, and *"love"* rather than negative words like *"hate"*. The crystals are beautiful and very unique. Words like, *"I will kill you"* and *"you fool"*, have a totally opposite effects on the water crystals. The crystals are not beautiful any more when using negative words on the water. Pictures were also taken of frozen water both before and after a Buddhist prayed and the difference is amazing. These beautiful pictures prove to us the effects negative thoughts and words have on our body. We literally change the structure of the water. When I read about the study the first time I was very surprised and a bit shocked. Do you know why I had that reaction?

Let me tell you why. I know that the human body is about 70% water and I have been around plenty of negativity throughout my life. I even thought it was cool to use negative curse words during my teenage years. When I read about the research I thought to myself, *"wow, what have I been doing to my vibrational energy through the water in my body all these years?""How many times have I been creating bad vibratory reactions due to bad language or negative thoughts?"* But after a while I calmed down and realized that water also has the power of adapting, the form is not solid so it does not matter how you have been treating the vibratory state of your body in the past. All that matters is the NOW and what you do from now on. How will you use this information to benefit you and your children? You can use words to change the energy vibration in your body and your children's body as well. Yes, you absolutely can, it's just a matter of making that decision. We have proof of the effects we can have, with simple words and thoughts. Imagine if you thought about the effects you have on the environment every time you speak, would you speak like you do today or would it be different? Would you change how you respond to your children, what you say to them, especially when you are disciplining them, knowing the effects of negative energy?

What about music, can music affect our vibrational energy levels? When Dr. Emoto put music on before freezing the water, the effects were amazing as well, nothing like the other results but beautiful all the same, just like when using words like *"love"* and *"respect"* for example. There were a lot of differences in the results on the water crystals depending on the music. Classical and soft music has very different effects than heavy metal for example.

I encourage you to look up online some of the pictures of the water crystals, they are very easy to find on the internet and you will see how beautiful some are and others not so beautiful depending on what energy vibration was applied to them. It is amazing how music can change the vibrational state of the water as well. Mankind has created a lot of music that makes people feel good, and now you know that it is because of the music's ability to change your vibrational state. Have you ever wondered why listening to certain music always makes you feel great? Well, now you know why!

What we say to our children and how we say it, will make a difference in both their and our well-being. We talked about changing your not wants into desirable goals in a chapter three, how to choose the positive way of saying things, and how to think in a positive way, to help us reach our goals. Do you think that the water crystal research, conducted by the late Dr. Emoto, supports that advice?

CHOOSE YOUR WORDS CAREFULLY

Would you like to know how to help your children even further? How to make them virtually limitless by working directly on their subconscious level?

Let me tell you a story about a man who helped his son, Blair, who was born without ears, unable to hear. This man was Napoleon Hill, who is probably most famous for writing the book *Think and Grow Rich*. Napoleon Hill was an inspiring man who changed lives all over the globe and his legacy still continues today to inspire and change people's lives. When his son Blair was born without ears, Napoleon knew the power of the subconscious mind and decided to help his son to hear. Blair was diagnosed with bilateral-microtia, a condition that causes children to be born with both ears either deformed or absent. Napoleon Hill had a burning desire for his son to hear, and, as he teaches us, the first step in changing your reality starts with a burning desire. He knew at that moment he would be able to help him, he just did not know how, but he knew the universe would show up with the solution as he was determined to help his son. He did a combination of many small things to help Blair to hear. One of them was that he would sit by his bed each night and talk to Blair's subconscious mind as Blair slept. To make the story short, Blair was able to hear at 60% of a normal level of hearing via bone conduction and later on in his life he was introduced to an acoustician hearing aid which enabled him to hear at 100% of normal hearing levels. Blair spent his life changing people's lives as well, just like his father, using the birth defect as an asset, which is exactly what it became when he started to help people around the world who could not before, to hear and speak.

What will you tell your child as you sit by the bedside while your child sleeps, what great gift will you sneak inside the subconscious mind of your child? Being limitless, being grateful, being thankful, being in the receiving state of mind for money to be attracted into his/her life or do you have something else in mind? What will you choose to condition into the subconscious mind of your child's life? The only limit is your imagination.

Will you choose your words more carefully from now on, when you talk to your children? Do you think the law of attraction does or does not apply to you? Do you think it matters what state of vibrational energy you live in?

If not, then maybe gravity does not apply either? Let me correct you if you think that. The laws of gravity and attraction, both work regardless of what you believe, they are laws that apply to you, regardless if you believe or not. You can choose to use them to your advantage or not!

THINK POSITIVE THOUGHTS

Do you think it makes a difference in your children's life, if you teach them how to think in a positive way? For example, your child comes to you and says that she is tired of not having anything new, like the other kids. The child might be influenced by the fact that someone at school just got something new, like a bike or a phone. Maybe the other children made fun of your child because she did not have anything new like the other, so called, cool kids. What are you going to tell your child, how can we turn that into a positive experience?

Maybe we have to talk about the things that we do have. Maybe we have to teach them to be thankful for something else. Maybe we can talk to them about our health. What do you think? The reason why I ask you is because there is no one way to do this right, and all children respond to different stories and messages. What will work on your children, that might not work on my children, just start trying different things out today. Don't wait. Start and find what works best. You are so powerful and you are so creative, that I am positive you will find a perfect way if you just start trying. The creative power sits inside of you waiting for you to bring it to life.

One of the most famous inventors of all time is Nikola Tesla who is probably most known for his gift to the world with AC electricity, the X-ray and the radio signals. All these three inventions are being used all over the world today. One thing that Tesla was obsessed with was frequency and he experimented with it a lot. One story tells of his experiment in New York when he found the right frequency for a building and shook the whole building almost to the point of breaking it. The radio signal works like this, if you send a certain frequency and set a receiver to the same frequency, you can send and receive signals. One night Tesla had a dream about his mother and when he woke up he was sure that she had passed away, which was the case. He realized that if two people are on exactly the same frequency they can connect with each other. When someone you know suddenly pops into your mind and you later find out that this same person was thinking about you at that exact time, is an example of two people being on the same frequency. It is common for twins, for example, to be on the same frequency. Me and my mother had this connection for the first 20 years of my life, she always knew if something bad happened to me. One example of that is 1998 when I was sick in the US and she was in Iceland. She asked my dad; *"What is wrong now?"* This happened exactly at the same time as I was diagnosed with a brain tumor. The strange thing about that incident was that from the minute I knew what was wrong I knew everything would be OK, and I do mean I really, really knew without a doubt. Everything worked out perfectly and the tumor is completely gone.

When you shift your frequency or your energy vibration to a higher state with some of the methods discussed in this book you might become aligned with someone you have not been aligned with before. Since you are going to a higher state of energy vibration you will start to attract new things and people into your reality.

ENERGY IS EITHER PUSHING OR PULLING

This means that if you are not growing you're essentially dying. I recommend to you, if you want to start working at a higher frequency, to change your language, use better, more positive, and more beautiful words to say the same thing. By doing that, you will change your vibrational state of being and you will shift either into or closer to alignment with your success story that you have already begun to write. The higher your energy vibration is the easier it is for you to achieve your goals.

Changing your mindset is a great way to shift your energy vibration to snap into alignment with your goals. I choose my words very carefully today, when I do my mindset work, when I think about stuff, when I talk to people, or even when I am writing something.

SUMMARY

Energy is everywhere.

Energy can neither be created nor destroyed, but it can be changed.

Your energy vibration changes according to your positive and/or negative words and thoughts.

When everything feels right and you feel great, you are most likely in alignment with your true purpose or goal.

We impact our environment greatly by our energy vibration and frequency.

Two people can be very connected if they are at the same frequency.

CHAPTER 10. CHANGING YOUR TUNE AND ENERGY VIBRATION

Can you hear all the music playing where you are right now? Trust me there is a very high probability that there is a lot of music where you are right now.

Don't believe me? OK, then! Let me prove it, take out a radio and turn it on, go through all the frequencies and you will hear all kinds of music, of course depending on where you are when reading this, but most likely a lot of music, a lot of radio stations. So what happened, did you pull the music into the room or was the music already there? It was already there, you were just listening to the wrong frequency.

When you drive your children to school, or anywhere else for that matter, what radio station do you listen to? This is a metaphorical question, we all know that the radio is being used less and less and we select what we listen to more and more with each year passing. Now we can connect our phones to the car radio, we have CD's; we have MP3 players and many other means of playing what we like to listen to. But in this example we will use the radio to illustrate a point. What radio station do you listen to when you are driving with your kids? The answer does not really matter, but what does matter is that whatever radio station you choose, your kids will listen to the same tune, the same frequency as you are listening to. This is what happens in life when we raise our children. They are automatically tuned into our frequency. Our frequency and our reality therefore becomes their frequency and their reality.

If you know that your frequency or your energy vibration is not giving you the results in life that you truly want, then why would you want your children listen to that same station, that same frequency? What do you need to do, to tune their frequency to a new, better, and more efficient station, to a higher frequency in life? You need to change your own frequency and influence our children that way.

WE NEED TO CHANGE OUR ENERGY VIBRATION.

Our bodies are conductors. We know scientifically that water can conduct electricity, for example. We also know that our body is made out of approximately 70% water. We, therefore must conclude that our bodies can conduct electricity. Electricity is a vibrational state of energy; therefore we know that we can conduct energy through our bodies. We also know that energy cannot be destroyed, it can only be converted into another state of vibration. We can use our bodies to conduct energy from the universe, the energy that has always has been here and is in everything we know as our reality. We can use that energy however we like. Whether you want to or not, you were made to channel the energy and be as one with it in different forms of vibrational states. Depending on your thoughts and actions you shift your energy vibration into higher or lower frequencies.

If you have decided, based on your current results in life, that it is time for you to change the channel and start conducting energy in a more efficient vibrational state, you need to learn

CHAPTER 10. CHANGING YOUR TUNE AND ENERGY VIBRATION

how. Are you ready to let go of what you think you know and let in new methods, rituals, and habits that have already been proven to work by other people, giving them the desired results they want in their lives?

Let's look at an example of a person who wanted to do just that.

A man walked up to a great master of martial arts. This master was Bruce Lee. The man asked Bruce Lee; *"can you teach me your ways?"* Bruce Lee replied to him kindly and said; *"yes I can, but first let me ask you a question."* The man replied and said; *"yes of course."* *"Can you remove what you think are the right methods and make room for my methods?"* said Bruce Lee, then he sat down at a table, reached for a glass and poured a dark soda drink, some kind of cola into the glass. He reached for another glass and filled it with pure clean water. He then placed the glasses side by side and told the man;

"This glass, with the cola, represents what you know, your wisdom. And this glass represents my knowledge", pointing to the other glass. *"Look at your glass, there is no room for my knowledge in there. Are you willing to empty your glass so you can fit my wisdom in your glass?"*

If you are ready to change the radio station, you must be ready to stop listening to your old favorite station. Are you ready? Are you willing to not judge the methods that have been proven to work for others, committing yourself to trying them and seeing your current results change by adapting these rituals? What steps will you take today to start changing your frequency and your children's frequency as well?

The time to start implementing these strategies into your life is now, as they mean nothing if you don't start right away. It all starts with a decision.

Here is a list of nine things you should stop doing to make room for the new methods. If none of these apply, you are most likely well off already on your journey to success. Start implementing some of these right now, today. All it takes to start, is to decide to start.

Give up the...

    complaints

    limiting beliefs

    blaming others

    negative self-talk

    dwelling in the past

    resistance to change

    need to impress others

    need to always be right

    need for approval from others

Your frequency will start to shift immediately when you start working on these. You should be feeling the change already, because it started the minute you started reading this book. You made a decision to seek knowledge and learn to implement new ideas and rituals into your life. Your glass is full of something you believe from your past. You must be willing to make room for new ideas and methods to be able to start shifting your frequency.

Like most people, I have experienced both high and low frequency in my life. Late 2012 I read a book that changed my life and opened my eyes to the world in a different way. Maybe it was because I was at a very low point in my life when I read the book, that it had such a massive impact on my life, or maybe I was just ready. I read the book Rich Dad, Poor Dad. Before that time I had only read one book, apart from the books I had glanced at or used to look up materials relevant to my schooling.

I almost read the whole book in one sitting and I was so open for change at that moment, maybe because my glass was completely empty at that time. I had seen all my efforts to become successful, fail. I had failed so many times that I felt like, this was it, I was done. What should I do, what could I do? When I finished the book, my frequency was raised through the roof. I started looking for more materials to read online and somehow, without being able to explain how, I accidentally signed up for Rich Dad coaching online, without knowing what coaching was or what I was signing up for. The next day a person from the Rich dad foundation called me, I was in Florida at the time. I answered and the man told me that I had signed up to begin my coaching at the Rich Dad foundation. I was in such a good frequency, my energy was high and without thinking about it, I said; *"Yes, that's right."*

One thing lead to another, I got through the first screening interview and was told that I would get a call from a coach the next day and that my spouse had to be interviewed as well. We had no money, lived on credit cards, and our business had failed in such a dramatic way that we were in a foreign country with no money at all. The next day we did the interview and then the big question came from me, how much would it cost. If I remember correctly it was $6.000 dollars, or very close to it, for 3 months of coaching. I asked if we could make payments and yes, we were allowed to do so. I paid the last $2.000 of our credit limit for the coaching. I studied all the materials I could get my hands on, showed up for the daily live meetings online, and when we had to pay the next $2.000, I called the Rich Dad foundation and told them I had lost my job and would have to drop out.

I spent the next 9 months of my life creating my first financial literacy course based on their materials and a few other books I read following the coaching. I have been on my journey to success since and today my life has completely changed. I read about one book every other week now, on self-improvement, mindset work, law of attraction, and other topics I find relevant to keep growing. I have coaches helping me every step of the way now. I live in a high state of energetic vibration today and most of my days, of course I have seen a few low frequency days, they are however, slowly but surely getting close to extinction. With each little step I take learning new mind

CHAPTER 10. CHANGING YOUR TUNE AND ENERGY VIBRATION

blowing things about how to reach my goals in life, I often think to myself; *"why did I not learn that in school, why did I not learn that in my childhood?"* Today, I implement everything I come across and think will help me to grow, in my daily life and I do grow each day. Each time, I think about how I can teach my children what I am learning and this book is the result of my transformation and my constant questioning of where I would be today if I had learned this as a child.

I have been following great speakers all over the world, one of whom I look up to in particular. In looking for ways to give back, I recently did something that felt right but did not turn out like I thought it would. I sent that person a message telling him that I noticed repeated word use in one of his messages and that it might be taking the focus of the great messages he was sharing. I spent about 3 hours one morning on analyzing the video, instead of spending my time on writing this book, because I believed that this was in alignment with my tune. Giving advice that I would welcome in my life, because I believe in treating others like you want to be treated yourself. The person got angry, called me names, and even though this was sent as a private message he decided to make an example out of me in front of all his followers the next day. He explained that I was this and that, called me names, and talked down to me in a video that was covering the topic of making people feel good about themselves, a little contradiction in his message. Do you see the irony there?

This influenced me greatly for some time and I allowed his reaction to shift my frequency to a lower frequency. I felt terrible for three days. I immediately took responsibility for my actions, repeating these words, both to myself and out loud; *"I love you, I am sorry, please forgive me and thank you."* I worked even harder than before on my mindset and projections towards my goals. I meditated for over 6 hours during the next three days and on the third day my frequency finally snapped back into alignment. At that moment I realized that my actions helped me in choosing my next coach. Before my *"mistake"*, I had decided to ask this person to coach me, but thankfully his reactions gave me exactly what I needed to know, that he was not the right coach for me. His reactions did not make him any less or more of a coach in my mind, only that he was not the right coach for me.

I have had coaches like him throughout my life, when I played sports, both during the 18 years I played basketball and the 3 years I played rugby. I apologized for my actions and truly felt sorry for what I had done. It was not my place to do that, but what I got back was exactly what I needed to keep growing as a person.

You should never be afraid to make mistakes but when you do, you need to own your mistakes and take total responsibility. What you might take from this example is, that if you are at a frequency which is in alignment with your true purpose and goals, you might sometimes do things that feel right, and get exactly what you need back from that action, even though it might not seem right at that point. We do not always get back what we think we will get back. If it feels right and you are living in the right state of frequency you will get back exactly what you need to move closer to your goals, to keep growing, keep moving forward. Listen to your intuition, you gut. Living in a state of high energy frequency and listening to your gut will get you amazing results.

SUMMARY

If you don't like your current results in life, start shifting your energy, and changing the channel. If you don't change, nothing will change.

Your current energy vibration is what you are currently teaching your children.

If you are willing to adopt new ideas and methods into your life, you have to make room to be able to fit them, empty your glass before you fill it with new wisdom and knowledge.

Work from a higher frequency to attract your desired goals into your reality.

Do whatever feels right and whatever it takes to keep growing each day; within the boundary of the laws of society, of course. You don't need to break any laws to move forward!

CHAPTER 11. BRAIN POWER AND HEALTH

What are the benefits of intermittent fasting, vigorous exercise, and cognitive challenges? What will I and my children benefit from it?

Each year the population of earth is aging, people are getting older, we live longer lives. With aging we run into new challenges, that we have to solve, or even better yet, prevent. One of the problems the human race is facing is the increasing number of Alzheimer's patients and obese people. According to the National Institute of Aging in the US, around 5 million people suffer from Alzheimer's disease today and it's projected to increase to 15 million by the year 2050. Mark Mattson shared the finding in a research he was part of, during a TEDx Talk at Johns Hopkins University, where he explained that what happens in the brain at later stages in life, is an accumulation of amyloid and damage to dopamine producing neurons. He and his team members found that the easiest way to extend the life of laboratory animals is to reduce their energy intake. By doing only that, the lifespan of the animals was extended by around 30-40%. There are two ways of decreasing the energy intake, one by eating smaller amounts each time, the other is intermittent fasting (reducing the frequency of the meals).

FASTING HAS GREAT BENEFITS TO THE MIND AND BODY.

"I fast for greater physical and mental efficiency."

Plato

Over 6.000 years ago, inside the pyramids in Egypt, this was written; *"Humans live on one-quarter of what they eat, on the other three quarters lives their doctor."*

WHAT DOES FASTING DO FOR THE BODY?

It reduces inflammation and oxidative stress in the body. The greatest thing fasting does is probably that it shifts your energy metabolism so your body starts using your fat to create energy, and when the body uses your fat it create ketone bodies in your liver. Think about it, how many obese people, who fast regularly, have you seen? When we eat the body stores the energy in the liver in the form of glycogen. That is the storage we always tap into first, but about 10-12 hours later you deplete the glycogen storage in your liver if you have not had any food during that period to produce more glycogen. When people eat throughout the day they usually never deplete the glycogen supply.

There is another way to deplete the glycogen, and that is when people train the body vigorously. Vigorously, meaning that you put your body under a lot of physical stress, but the good kind of stress of pushing yourself.

What happens in the body when you deplete the glycogen storage? Your body starts to burn fat, turning it into ketone bodies. Ketone bodies are very good for your brain. There are numerous ways of fasting and intermittent fasting is becoming very popular these days. One example of intermittent fasting is to restrict your energy intake to 8 hours, which is long enough to shift your energy metabolism – the other 16 hours you only drink water. I personally fast for about 16-20 hours once a week, were I only drink water during that period. You can look up the many different ways to be able to shift your energy metabolism through intermittent fasting and start creating ketone bodies.

The great impact fasting has on your brain, is believed to be caused by brain stress (the good kind). The body thinks it is not getting food and starts to produce ketone bodies, which your brain uses, from your fat, increases your brain power, you become more alert and more energetic. To understand this reaction better we can apply it to the history of evolution where the response of the body, not getting food, is to create a state of having to find food, go out and hunt. The brain can easily substitute glycogen for ketone bodies, even though he prefers glycogen. The body does absolutely not want the brain to shut down, but to be able to figure out how to find more food we need more brain power. When the human brain is being supplied ketone bodies, the brain functions better.

This does not apply to most of us today, because we can access food anytime we want, but nevertheless this is still the response of the body when we fast. Your nerve cells become more active. The same thing happens in your brain with vigorous exercise. Have you noticed how good you feel after a hard workout? Your mood becomes better and you are relaxed, and yet you become more energetic by exercising vigorously on a regular basis.

Intermittent fasting and exercise both increase the production of proteins in the brain, called neurotrophic factors. This increase in production of neurotrophic factors promotes the growth and connections of neurons and strengthen the synapses in your brain.

Cognitive challenges is another thing we can do to have the same effects on the brain, when we challenge our brain by solving problems or learning new things.

Is there any other way to get ketone bodies for your brain? If, for any reason, you can't fast, vigorously exercises or challenge your brain, there is another way to produce ketone bodies. Dr. Mary Newport turned her husband's Alzheimer's around, well not completely but significant improvements were recorded. When she started to learn about Alzheimer's she found that the Alzheimer's disease is a type of brain diabetes. The brain starts to have problems with insulin, preventing brain cells to accept glucose and, as a result, the brain cells start dying. This usually starts around 20 years before symptoms start to show.

What she did to reverse the process was to start giving her husband coconut oil, which helps the liver to produce ketone bodies. She emphasized that you must make sure that the coconut oil is non-hydrogenated. Ketone bodies are easily accepted as an alternative fuel for the brain cells. Although this was discovered as a partial cure, the best way is always to prevent things from happening in the first place. That's where exercise, intermittent fasting, and cognitive challenges work wonders.

Intermittent fasting, exercise, and cognitive thinking can also increase the production of new nerve cells from stem cells in at least one region of your brain, called the hippocampus. The Romans discovered that people with epilepsy, who they considered back then to be possessed by demons, could be thrown into a room and by not being fed, the demons would go away. Today we know that this was due to the effects ketone bodies have on the brain. Today, some doctors still use Ketone diets to treat epilepsy for the known fact that ketone bodies suppress seizures.

Intermittent fasting also increases the number of mitochondria in your nerve cells, similar effects are seen when weightlifting and increasing the number of mitochondria in your muscles. By increasing the mitochondria in the brain you can produce more energy and increase your ability to learn and memorize things. Another scientifically proven benefit from fasting is the enhanced ability of your nerve cells to repair your DNA.

Exercise, intermittent fasting, and cognitive challenges can ensure you and your children live healthier and longer lives.

Your children absorb everything you do and if you decide to try out any of the many ways to do intermittent fasting, apply it to your children as well, as long as you are not doing fasting for a longer period than 12-24 hours each time. If you have not been fasting or exercising in the past, I will always recommend taking baby steps. Intermittent fasting can cause some strain on your body and mind if you go too fast into changing your eating habits, just like going to the gym for the first time does. You could, for example, decide to use the 8 hours a day intermittent fasting one day per week. Later you might increase it to two days per week. You might decide that eating within an 8 hour period would be most suitable for you and your family, and that's perfect, do what you think is right. It would be a shame not to implement this in any way into your life, because we now have scientific proof of the health benefits, as well as the preventative benefits and long term benefits.

Encourage your children to feed their brain by learning new things, playing chess or building Lego's for example. Encourage your children to exercise in the form of playing. You can also find information online about how to exercise with your children as participants in your workouts if you are interested to do so. It can be a very fun way to do your exercises.

Prevention is always better than a cure. Stay healthy and full of energy to be able to take action on the transformation you want to see in your life and your children's lives.

SUMMARY

Intermittent fasting increases your brain power and keeps you healthier.

Vigorous exercising help depleting your glycogen storage, encouraging your body to start producing ketone bodies, which are very good source of energy.

Cognitive challenges help your brain to stay in shape, so to speak, increase your brain power, and increase your ability to learn and memorize things.

CHAPTER 12. SEEDS OF GRATITUDE

What kind of seeds have you been planting your whole life?

What kind of seeds do you plan on planting in your children's garden?

Is gratitude one of the seeds you plant each day?

There is a time to put seeds into the ground and there is a time to harvest, this is true in almost all aspects of life! It means that when we prepare something or start a new ritual to transform our lives in any way, we start by planting new seeds in our garden. Sometimes we see the harvest or the results right away but in other cases we must stay on course and keep planting the seeds, the harvest might take longer than expected at first. This depends on the task at hand, what transformations are you implementing in your life and what are the results you seek?

We usually have the two standard seasons per year, spring for planting and fall for harvesting. Is it possible for us to increase the harvest, or better yet, is it possible for us to increase the number of seasons to plant and harvest within a single year?

Yes we can. It is done with habits and rituals. When we implement good rituals which become good habits, we create greenhouse conditions in our lives, we can harvest in the winter, summer, spring or fall. This is something we can do with mindset exercises, goal settings, goal achievements, self-improvement training, and transitioning into who we need to become. This also applies to how we raise our children, we can teach them to harvest more often than those who do not practice any mindset work at all. We can teach our children to manifest anything they desire with rituals which turn into good habits. We can teach our children to lead by example, we can even teach our children to teach us new things in life!

Maybe this is hard to imagine, that we can teach our children to teach us. Here is an example of how you can do this. My daughter and I start every day together with a gratitude ritual. This can be a fun and easy way to start your day. You can decide to do this at the breakfast table or even in the car on your way to dropping the kids off at school. You should start by explaining the ritual to your children, what you are about to do.

You could say something like; *"Do you want to play a really fun game?"* Kids love to have fun and play games. Remember to be in a state of good vibration, starting this ritual only when everything is in good balance, don't try and start this ritual right after a fight, when the children are frustrated, in a bad mood, or extremely tired. Starting the ritual in a good vibration makes it much easier to continue the next day, as the children will associate it with a good feeling. When starting, you lead by example, saying out loud what you are grateful for. At first, while implementing the ritual into your and your children´s lives name three things your children can relate to. If you currently don't do a daily gratitude ritual and you have a hard time thinking about things to be grateful for in the beginning, start with something simple like, for example;

"I am grateful for having such wonderful children.

I am grateful that we all woke up this morning.

I am grateful for being able to spend time with my children.

I am grateful for being able to breathe.

I am grateful for being alive.

I am grateful for being able to say what I am thankful for this morning with my children."

Next have your children say three things they are grateful for. If they don't start on their own you could help them by leading them to something you know they are truly grateful for. Give your children several days and they are likely to surprise you with what they'll think of. They can actually start teaching you things about them or yourself. This is one example of you teaching your children to teach you. You will learn a lot about them too through this exercise, what they are grateful for, how they think, and what they value in life at their age.

SOWING SEEDS

When you grew up, you were influenced by your parents and you started to sow seeds in your garden, knowingly or not. The same thing is happening with your children right now, they are starting their garden by planting seeds influenced by you, your actions, and what you teach them.

You might have noticed at some point in your life, that you have been planting orange seeds all along and all you have harvested so far in life are orange trees and oranges. This is of course metaphorically speaking, meaning that whatever effort you have put in or what you have been taught through conditioning from your parents have led to the results you have today. Maybe you woke up one day and said to yourself; *"I don't want to be like my parents."* I know most of us feel so at some point in time, about something that our parents do or did, which we do not want to repeat or become. Upon realizing this one of two things might have happened, you either realized you don't know how to plant any other kind of seeds or you started to seek information on how to plant different kinds of seeds in your garden. You could have, for example, wanted to plant apple seeds to be able to harvest apple trees and apples. Did you find out how or are you still seeking the information and rituals needed to change the type of seeds you plant?

You are already changing what you plant in your garden just by reading this book and implementing the exercises, routines, and methods I am sharing with you. You do not have to implement all of the rituals and methods right away. You can start with the ones you like the most and think will be the most fun. Once those have become your daily routine or habits read the book again and find new rituals and exercises to implement. At this point you will have started harvesting from the new seeds you planted before in your and your children's gardens. Your garden has no boundaries, the more you sow the more you harvest. Your garden can grow way beyond what you realize today.

If you want to be in the top 1% of parents raising top 1% children, take as many of these simple rituals you can and implement them into your life, into your daily routine. You are meant to grow throughout your life and that is why the metaphor of seeds and harvest is so relevant in your life.

Leaving a legacy behind for your children is like planting seeds in a garden you will never see grow but knowing that the garden will keep on growing and blooming long after your work in it is done.

SUMMARY

Knowing what you have been planting in your garden, gives you the insight to change what you have been sowing and harvest new kinds of results in your life.

Gratitude rituals are a part of stepping into the identity you need to be, to be able to grow faster and further than your wildest dreams.

Keeping your children involved in your transformation will make the transformation more fun and more powerful, for both you and your children.

CHAPTER 13. FEELINGS ARE NEITHER RIGHT NOR WRONG

What causes feelings?

Why is it important for us to listen to our children when they share their feelings?

Why is it important for us to make no judgment when our children or spouse are sharing their feelings?

Can we influence what is triggering those feelings?

When raising children it is important to realize that feelings are neither right nor wrong. When your children tell you how they feel, the only thing you need to say is; *"thank you for sharing that."* Those same reactions are even common in our relationships, when our spouse is sharing how he/she feels, and sometimes we make the situation worse, leading to our own energy vibration shifting to a lower frequency. We might feel that our spouse should not feel that way and we react by showing emotions like anger, sadness or fear. Understanding that feelings are neither right nor wrong will help us understanding the cause of the feelings, as they are only the symptoms of a trigger, usually triggered by a belief. If we want to help our children to shift their energy vibration and bring forth new, positive, and happy feelings, we need to realize what is actually causing these feelings, what is the belief trigger.

One of the best lessons in my life has been, to learn to listen and simply thank people for sharing their feelings. If a person would ask you for help regarding a certain feeling, then we need to look at what is causing that particular feeling. Most of the time just by sharing what you are feeling, you shift your vibrational energy and fix the trigger yourself. Once you have the understanding to listen without judgment you will see how most of the unnecessary emotional arguments in your life will slowly fade away.

WHAT IS THE CAUSE OF FEELINGS AND EMOTIONS?

The cause is almost always what we believe so to influence or change our feelings we need to reprogram our limiting beliefs. This is why it is very important for us to realize that feelings are simply responses to our belief system, pure and simple, neither right nor wrong.

Listening honestly without judgment as a parent will play a big role for your children, especially when they become teens. Imagine if, by the time your children become teens and the hormones start to influence their lives in a big way as when you went through puberty, they are able to confide in you and share their feelings knowing that they will not be judged. When I was a teen I could go to my mom when I had a hard time or was heartbroken, and all she did was listen to me and comfort me. I was pretty lucky to have a dad for mental growth and a mom whom I could share my defeats with. Be willing to let go of judgment and be there for your children when they want to share their feelings, just listen to them, might prevent all kinds of unnecessary troubles for them. You will learn more about yourself as parent and your children when they can openly share their feelings. I believe the only way to not be judgmental, is to remind ourselves as often as we need to, that feelings are not right and not wrong.

It is not always easy to find what belief is causing that particular feeling but if we talk about the circumstances that caused it, we start to get closer to the truth, the cause. If you are talking to your child about the situation, it is very important to keep asking the right questions, as the child will eventually tell you what beliefs are causing those feelings.

Let's play out an imaginary scenario to illustrate how a parent could possibly find the belief trigger behind a feeling.

Your child comes home from school one day, very sad and tells you that the day was terrible.

Child; *"I feel so sad, it was a terrible day at school."*

Parent; *"Thank you for sharing that with me."*

Child; *"I don't want to feel this way."*

Parent; *"Do you want to tell me what happened at school?"*

Child; *"I saw the boys picking on Johnny, and they were very mean to him."*

Parent; *"Did that make you sad?"*

Child; *"Yes."*

Parent; *"What did you do?"*

Child; *"Nothing."*

Parent; *"Why?"*

Child; *"Because I don't want to get hurt, they are strong boys."*

Parent; *"Did you want to do something to help?"*

Child; *"Yes, but what can I do?"*

Parent; *"You have several ways to help, you could have asked them to quit, you could have ran to fetch an adult to stop the bullying or asked the crowd to stop this. Most of the time we have several options to choose from, and doing nothing is also a choice."*

Child; *"I thought about it."*

Parent; *"Do you want to start making a difference in other people's lives?"*

Child; *"Yes, but I am so busy at school and working on my own stuff."*

Parent; *"Is there any other reason you don't want to impact your surroundings but instead only focus on yourself?"*

Child; *"You are always saying we need to take care of ourselves first; no one else will help us."*

This was an imaginary situation, but could easily be real. The reason I picked this situation as an example, is because my biggest mental block in the past was to believe that I would have to do everything myself. By talking about the feelings and how they were triggered, the parent found that the belief system the child was holding on to, came from the parent, which is the case most of the time. The child believed that it should not intervene in other people's lives because of a conditioned belief, from being raised to believe that we need to take care of ourselves and no one else.

To change our belief system in this particular imaginary example, we would have to change our beliefs and the child's as well. As parents we would have to change the belief that we only need to focus on ourselves and do everything ourselves. We have to be willing to accept help, and give help. This example is a perfect scenario to get your child involved in your own transformation, to change both your and your child's beliefs. I know that when you start to teach your children the right way of thinking, influence how they manifest their dreams, help them become more grateful and so on, you will benefit the most yourself as parent.

We have covered two different methods on how to change your subconscious beliefs, referring to earlier chapters in this book to use in a situation like this one. Both you and your children will benefit right away at the same scale, after which the children can start teaching someone else to do the same. You become a role model and start truly living in your powerful new identity, when you reach the place of being able to teach others. In this scenario it would be a great idea to start giving, volunteering, or donating with your children, letting your children experience the true joy of giving, helping others, and influencing your environment in a positive way. This might be enough to change your children's beliefs, while you would probably need to work a little bit more on your own beliefs because they have deeper roots.

SUMMARY

Feelings are neither right nor wrong.

Feelings are almost always triggered by something that you believe.

Don't try to fix the feelings, try to find the belief that triggered the feeling.

We can reprogram our belief system to prevent that belief triggering the state of emotion we don't want to experience.

Being able to listen to your children sharing their feelings without judgment will bring you closer together as a family and later as friends.

CHAPTER 14. FUN LESSONS

A SIMPLE AND VERY POWERFUL MONEY MINDSET RITUAL FOR YOU AND YOUR CHILDREN

Here is an exercise for you and your children to do together. This is a fun and powerful ritual. It will shift your money mindset, boost your growth to success, and teach your children the power of giving. According to Tony Robbins, when you start giving is the time you start receiving. If you cannot afford to give 10 cents of a dollar today, then you will absolutely not be able to afford to give $10,000,000 out of your $100,000,000. Regardless of your wealth, your scarcity mindset will stay the same if you don't change it right away. This is why you should start giving now, stepping into the identity you need to be and start experiencing the mindset of abundance.

Start by finding three piggy banks or anything of equal size, it can be literally anything, use your imagination. When I started this exercise with my children I used glass jars as seen on the following picture.

Label your piggy banks with; *"spending/fun money"*, *"savings"*, and *"charity"*. I labeled mine on the lids, which are underneath the jars in the picture.

> The spending or fun money jar, is the jar you and your children will use for anything you like, movies, going out to dinner, or anything that gives you joy. This, for example, would be an excellent jar to use to celebrate your little wins on the journey to becoming the best parent you can be.
>
> The savings jar is for the money you will keep, taking it to the bank regularly to deposit it into a savings account. By physically going to the bank together with your children allowing them to do the deposit under your supervision you create both a visual and practical experience for them, teaching them a valuable skill, one that will later become their habit.

The charity jar is the money you give to charity or a good cause each month, without asking for or expecting anything in return. This is in my opinion, the most important jar for you and your children. Let your children be involved in deciding each month where the money should go. Maybe you drive by a homeless man who your children ask about, you could ask them right back if they want to give this man the charity money this month. They might also decide to support a charity at their school or maybe you will find something both you and your children support, like an animal shelter. Maybe you want to adopt a child in Africa and give the fund to that child each month. Whatever you think is worth giving to and your children will want to stay involved with.

It is totally up to you how you start this ritual, how much you put in the jars each day, or if you do it weekly, you decide what works for you and your children. You could start with one dollar in each jar daily or $5 in each jar weekly. This means you'd be putting approximately $60-$90 in the jars per month, the amount you can then slowly increase as your success grows. Ideally you want the charity jar to end up representing 10% of what you bring home each month, but of course it's totally up to you, what you strive towards and what you can cope with. You might even start with putting only 25 cents in each jar, just remember it does not matter how small you start as long as you start, and the sooner you start the better. As soon as you start this ritual your whole family will shift their money mindset and start attracting more money into your lives.

METHOD TO MANIFEST DREAMS FOR YOU AND YOUR CHILDREN

Teach your children how to manifest their dreams into reality with this simple method.

Take a box of any kind, wood, cardboard, plastic, or from any other material. Put a label on it saying; *"What goes in becomes real."*

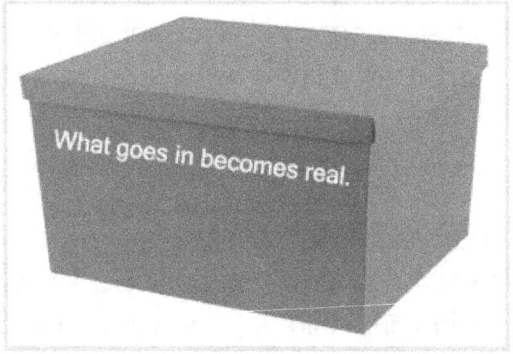

Now explain to your children how the box works. They take a picture of something they desire or write it on a piece of paper and place it in the box, for example a brand new red bike, which is what will be used to illustrate the method. They find a picture of a new red bike in a magazine for example, cut it out, drop it in the box, and close it. Next explain to your children that by putting the picture in the box they are a step close to getting that bike, it will be manifested into their reality, their life. Let them think about it overnight and tell them that you will explain how the magic works tomorrow. This is an important part to challenge their cognitive brain function and make them excited to find out more.

The day after you start by explaining how this box will manifest their dreams. You open the box together with your children, looking at the picture telling them that the next step is to find out how much the bike costs, maybe you go into a bike shop and find the bike and the price tag there or maybe you look online. Make sure your children participate in the journey the whole time. Once you have a price, let's say $150 to illustrate the method, you write that price on another piece of paper adding one third or 10% on top, we will use one third giving us total price of $200. Place this paper, and a jar for the charity donation to keep the money separated, in the box.

Next explain to your children that they need to think about ways to manifest that money into their reality. How will they earn that money? As a parent make sure you use a method which enables your children to contribute as much as possible to the project, to be an active participant in every step on the way. Here are a few examples;

> You could bake cookies and sell once a week in your neighborhood. You and your children can go knocking on doors telling your neighbors that they will be selling cookies to manifest money for their dream bike, making weekly rounds with the freshly baked products, and that they can make orders with them if they are interested. Once you have the orders then you and your children will go and bake the cookies together, remember to let your children participate as much as possible in the whole

process, taking orders, baking, deliveries and collecting payments. Each time you get a payment, place the money into the box and fix the price tag by subtracting the amount created that day, for example, if you made $10, subtract it from the original $200, writing the remaining $190 on the price tag, and tell your children how much is left to reach the goal.

Pick night crawlers from your yard or the park and sell to a fishing store or directly to anyone who is going fishing. The same thing applies, you and your children go together knocking on doors finding someone who wants to purchase night crawlers for fishing. Picking night crawlers is done simply by watering your lawn, waiting till it's dark to go out with a flashlight and pick those that have crawled up. I used to do this myself as a child.

Collect soda cans and sell them. If however, you can only redeem money in the form of a note that can be used at the grocery store where you are living, you will keep that note for yourself using it for groceries, replacing it with the equal amount of cash so that your children can put the money in the box. You can also go around the neighborhood finding people who do not save their cans and ask them to save them for your children to collect them each Sunday until the goal is reached.

Create a YouTube channel for your children and start making funny videos, or talent videos or anything interesting. You could record your children playing video games, if that is something they like to do, posting them online on the YouTube channel to start getting views and some advertisement revenue from that. You will of course have to supervise this. If you don't know how to do this, but are interested, you can easily find tutorials on YouTube that will teach you how to set everything up from scratch and how to monetize the videos.

Clean the cars in the neighborhood. Same principle applies, you go with your children and ask around who would like to get their car cleaned, for example, once a week for a reasonable price.

Another idea would be to offer paid chores around the house. These could be taking out the garbage each day, doing the dishes, getting the mail, vacuuming, or whatever you think will teach them both responsibility and the value of getting paid for service rendered. This, however, would not be my first option and I recommend if possible having the chore outside the house. I would only use this as an option if you feel the need to and can't possibly help them in any other way. The reason is that doing chores only teaches them to swap time for money but not how to treat customers or retailers, while the other activities mentioned before outside the house, can by multiplied, scaled up, and teaches them how to trade a scalable service for money. If they catch on, they could later hire someone else to do their work while taking home handsome profits just by supervising the activity. Another reason for why paying for house chores is not optimal, is that you don't get paid for it and it might seem strange paying them to do something you do for free. If however, you feel this is your only way to help them, you could have certain chores they do as part of their responsibility and therefore do not get paid for, but have other chores, those that don't need to get done every day, like raking leaves, or mowing the lawn, that you pay them for.

Regardless of what you decide to do, this will teach your children how to manifest their dreams into reality. You have to go on this journey with them, and yes, this will take some effort on both your and your children's behalf. It will be a very valuable lesson in mindset groundwork for your children's future success. When you have the total amount go with them and help them pay for the bike on their own, after which you let your children choose a charity or good cause to give the $50 to, they might even want to give this money to a homeless person. If that is what they want to use the charity money for, let them do it. If your children are not able to make the choice, set up a few charity ideas for them to select from, involve them in it as well, so that when your children deliver the charity money they will experience the joy of giving.

Have fun with it and you will be spending quality time with your children seeing how their personalities grow, and noticing that by teaching them this, they will appreciate that new red bike so much more than if you would just go out and buy it for them.

SUMMARY

Charity jar, fun jar, and savings jar will shift your money mindset.

Giving to charity will teach your children the joy of giving.

Teach your children visually and practically to manifest their dreams into reality with a simple exercise with a box.

Teach your child to take orders, be unafraid of knocking on doors with you by their side, and how to make money with scalable methods.

CHAPTER 15. RITUALS AND HABITS

We are the average sum of all our habits.

Habits are formed whether we try to form them or not.

Habits are a big part of our lives, whether we like it or not. When we think about habits, often we think about something that is intentionally practiced over time, like exercising or waking up early in the morning. What about all the habits we implement into our lives without knowing it? Have you ever put a belt on your pants the other way around, or which sock do you put on first, ever tried starting with the other? Try it next time and see how strong this simple habit is in your life. We have so many small habits we don't realize are actual habits. The addiction of cigarettes or tobacco is believed to be around 80% habit and 20% addiction. This is why it is easier for many people who, for example, decide to quit smoking, to implement that when they move to a new house. The new environment starts with a clean slate, like an empty piece of paper. We might realize that many of our habits are not linked to a place or an environment and that makes them a little bit harder to change. The first step is of course to identify the habits.

We need to be aware of our habits and our children's habits, if we want to be able to improve or adjust them.

Do you think you have any habits that you have never considered habits before? Do you have a ritual before taking a shower, when you wake up, before you go to sleep, before you go to work, after you come home in the evenings or before you eat dinner or lunch? You might realize that our lives are based on habits. When you realize that, you know the lives of your children will be the same as well. The more we teach them to consciously work on creating good positive habits, the less they will develop subconscious bad habits. I am referring to habits like, for example, not deciding something, yes, that can be a habit as well! You might know some people whose lives are led by such bad habits of not making any decisions, staying in the so called comfort zone. These people would never reach this part of the book for example, because of their habits of quitting or judging before evaluating for themselves. Thankfully you are not one of them. You reached this point, which means you are a person who takes action and evaluates the information presented to you, and most likely you will adopt a few of these suggestions, even the majority of them. You are not afraid to make decisions and take action.

Keep in mind that your children, while they are still young, don't have habits with deep roots so if there is something you would like to teach them or even change in their habits, it shouldn't be hard. The first e-book I wrote was about children's sleeping habits and how parents can easily change them. Most new parents, especially first time parents, bring home their child and are literally about to explode from love. For most first time parents it is also very natural, and perfectly fine, to make a few mistakes. Some of those mistakes can lead to bad habits but correcting them is not as hard as you might think, if you know how to. Let's take an example of bad sleeping habits new parents might develop. They come home from the hospital

CHAPTER 15. RITUALS AND HABITS

happy and excited, the mother is breastfeeding their new child. They start realizing it takes effort and hard work to have a new baby in the family, everything changes. The mother is quick to realize that she can actually read her favorite books while the baby is being breast fed, she just gets comfortable in the master bed and before she knows it she start looking forward to this time in the evenings. The baby falls asleep next to the warm mother's body after being fed. The mother thinks this is great and lets the baby sleep in the bed because it is so convenient, she loves the baby so much, and all the other perfect reasons for letting the baby just sleep next to mommy. The mother also realizes having the baby next to her is very convenient when it wakes up in the middle of the night wanting milk as she can feed it with minimum effort. You might notice how this is a bad habit forming.

Everything feels perfect for the first couple of months, but what are the consequences? The dad might delay his time going to bed as much as he can, the romance in the relationship is little to none and the baby cannot fall asleep unless mommy is there. This might continue for a few more months, in this example we will project that at around 7 months old when the baby is starting to reject mommy's milk and ready to eat solid food. At this time the baby's habit of sleeping in mommy's bed is getting pretty strong, but remember that even though the baby still does not know anything else, this can be fixed in as little as two days. I have helped parents transitioning a child from the master bed to their own in only two days. In one particular case the child was 2 years old and still sleeping in the master bed with mommy!

Here are a few steps you can take to transition your child from the master bed into their own.

> Make sure to have a transitional period for the sleep ritual itself, usually around 20 to 30 minutes before you want the child to be asleep. Like a basketball player who does the same thing each time before shooting a free-throw or a golfer who does the same practice swing before hitting a ball, you also must develop a pre-game ritual for your children so it becomes a habit to go to sleep at the same time each night. If your goal is to have the child go to sleep at 8pm you can develop an anchor around 7.30pm. This can be done in several ways, like telling them to put on the pajamas, saying it is 20 minutes until we brush our teeth giving them a chance to play a little longer, but knowing the wheels are in motion by now. Another way would be to touch the child in a way you do only at this moment of the day to trigger the anchor, maybe two hands on the shoulders and calmly say; *"it's time to put on your pajamas"*. There is really no wrong way of creating the anchor you want to use for your children's sleeping habits as long as you don't keep changing them.
>
> Make sure you watch the time to ensure you are following the pre-game ritual. Begin brushing their teeth after 20 minutes, or let them do it themselves if they are old enough. It is important to try to be as punctual as possible so that this ritual becomes a habit sooner than if you are always fluctuating the time. When they finish cleaning their teeth, go with them to their bed and tuck

CHAPTER 15. RITUALS AND HABITS 167

them in. At this point it is up to you whether you want to just say a prayer, read a book or simply just say goodnight to them. If you are transitioning the child into its own bed and its own room as well, there are a few things to have in mind for the transition to be as smooth as possible. First make sure the child has used the toilet before going to bed. Second make sure you stay close so you can hear the child at all times until the child falls asleep for the first few times in its new environment. Keep the door slightly open for easy access into the room when or if the child starts to cry, which most of them do the first night at least. Make sure you put their blanket tightly around their body when you tuck them in, but be careful not to cover the face of course. The reason this can help, is if the child is very young, it is comforting feeling to be tightly tucked in as they were their first 9 months of their lives in the belly. When or if the baby starts to cry go to the door show yourself if need be, then go all the way into the room and tell them that now it is time to go to sleep tucking them back into their cover. If it is enough for you just to talk calmly and tell your child to go to sleep through the slightly open door then that is preferable, if not then go into the room. The child might stand up and reach for you with tears in their eyes, but remember that under no circumstances should you pick the child up, the only exceptions are if the child is injured, sick, or needs to use the toilet. If the child needs to use the toilet take him/her there and help as needed, then take the child right back to bed, always talking calmly to him/her saying it is time to go to bed. If you have a very hard time the first night, try to step one step away from the bed each time you have to check on the child. Slightly tilt the door back and say good night kindly to your child. If the child is crying heavily you need to use a watch to follow a simple strategy. Let 60 seconds pass before entering the room the next time and then stop one step further away from the bed than you did last time, go outside and wait 2 minutes before taking action the next time and so forth. I have witnessed up to 5 hours the first night. But at the same time I have not seen any problems on the third night if you make sure to follow rule number one, do not take the child out of the bed. After 8pm the child is supposed to be in bed and that is the ritual you are implementing so it can become a habit.

Make sure you wake the child up at the same time each day. You can create a fun game to play in the morning or you can implement a ritual of saying things that you are grateful for. This part is really up to you. What do you consider is a great way to start your day and your children's day? One game you might consider is to give the child a sticker each morning if they did well the previous night and if they collect a certain number of stickers they can get a reward of some kind. Again, this is up to you.

Why would we want to transition our child from the master bed into their own, or why should we set up new sleeping rituals to get our child to go to bed at the same time each night? Sleep is essential to our survival and we all need sleep. Your children will be happier when they have a good sleeping ritual or habit, and so will you.

(*This example was a brief summary from the book Sleeping Habits and Routines, to see more visit http://HuniHunfjord.com*).

When we adopt rituals into our lives and stick to them long enough, they become habits. Habits are things we do without having to put any conscious thought to it, we simply do them. If you fail at adopting new rituals into your life, don't worry about it, just keep trying and don't give up. You walk around today without thinking about it, but at some point you did not know how to walk. How would the world be today if small children would consciously decide to stop trying when they fall the first few times trying to walk? Children are not born with the mentality of stop trying, that is a conditional behavior. You can condition a mindset of quitting. We can develop habits of not trying, but most of us don't realize that not trying or quitting can easily become a habit.

You might have noticed in today's society, that we often try to keep our children at the same level, meaning they might participate in a tournament of some sort, sports or any other activity, where no one wins and no one loses. We can easily build habits of not winning as well. I believe it is nice to give the children some token of appreciation for participating in an event but what are we teaching them if they only participate to participate and no one wins? Are we teaching them that they should not try to become better at anything? How could we inspire the less talented kids to improve themselves? I believe that we should be teaching them to improve their performance measured by their own accomplishments. Habits of hard work can almost always outweigh talents. How about simply measuring if they are improving? If we look at some sports where you only compete against yourself, like golf for example, you can easily track if or how you are improving and that is the only true measurement. The same would apply to chess or even at school, we do not need to measure our progress against others, the only thing we need to look at is whether we are improving or not, then we are on the right path. Have you ever seen a team that expects to lose each time they compete? What about a team that expects to win each time they compete? Have you noticed the differences in their records or stats?

HOW LONG DOES IT TAKE TO ADOPT A NEW HABIT?

Some say it takes 21 days of doing something every day to make it a habit. If you can stay on track with your new rituals for 21 days it is very likely you will succeed in making it a habit, but the truth is it takes longer than that to create a habit that will be a part of your new lifestyle. It could take up to 6 months to create a true habit. 21 days of doing the ritual is a great first milestone, because after 21 days it will be much easier to keep the momentum going.

Rituals of positive thinking for example will eventually become a habit and you will automatically think in a positive way were as you did not before. Many of your current habits are created by conscious decisions and some you adopt without thinking about it, like walking. If you pay attention to everything you do for one whole day, you will realize that you have multiple habits you did not even realize were actual habits. Do you like them all? Do you want to change any of them? These can be anything from how you shake hands with people, how you walk, how you comb your hair, how you eat, to how you think and react to different situations. If you keep this in mind you will start to noticing your, as well as your children's habits. You can change all your habits, if you want to.

COMPOUNDING EFFECTS OF HABITS WHEN RAISING A CHILD

The power of compounding happens by taking baby steps each time.

Darren Hardy wrote about habits and rituals in his book *The Compounding Effect* and if I were to explain the book in one sentence, I would say that, you need to make small daily changes which you stick to, and a few years from now you will see the effects of compounding these small changes over time as success in your life.

This is really relevant regarding how we raise our children. What small thing will you teach your children to implement into their routines and habits today that will make a difference in their lives 10 years from now?

> *"Success is not doing 5,000 things really well. Success is doing a half dozen things really well 5,000 times."*

Darren Hardy

Do your children brush their teeth before bed? How about when they wake up? Are they polite? Do they fuss over the dinner you cook? Do they thank you for the food? Do they offer to help you when you are doing something? Do they ask before borrowing things? Are they generally finishing the things they start or do they quit before they reap the benefits? Do they have any rituals that you do with them? Do they have a pre-game ritual or habits before bedtime? Do they have a morning ritual? Do they show up on time when they need to be somewhere?

These are just a few questions to help you think. Sometimes we let our children do things because we don't care, or maybe because we could not do a particular thing ourselves as children, or maybe because we believe we are just being nice to them. Whatever the reason might be, think about the possible consequences? Simple things, like not teaching our children to finish what they start, could easily become a habit of quitting. Most people who come from humble beginnings and manage to become great successful people in their adult life, agree that the only thing you need to avoid to succeed in life, is quitting.

The rituals we develop with our children will compound over time, and some of the rituals they do not enjoy at first, will become an essential part of their existence in the future and very enjoyable.

"I don't want to be a strict parent", someone might be thinking to themselves. We can find ways to implement rituals without applying force.

Let's say you are the type of a parent who never wants to tell their children what to do. Your children should be waking up early in the morning, but they have not been doing that and they are going to bed later than you have asked them to. One way for you to get them to wake up earlier would be to tell them that you are going to an amusement park in the morning and whoever goes to bed after 8pm will be responsible to get up on their own in the morning, they won't be woken up. The morning after you leave according to schedule regardless of who is awake by then, of course after making arrangements of an adult being around to watch over the children who slept in. I would never recommend you do anything that will jeopardize your children. You might explain to your parents, their grandparents, how you are using this method to teach your children a valuable lesson in life, and have them come over in the morning just in case someone does not wake up. This is just an example of one way to teach a valuable lesson in life about taking responsibility and listening to you when you tell them they need to go to bed before 8pm. This example will not affect the children unless they love the amusement park. This will only work if they miss out on something they love to do. I realize that many parents would never do this to their children. I believe we need to teach them in the way that we feel comfortable with, of course. Adversity is one of the best learning experiences a child can go through.

Most parents will just want their children listen and follow rules without teaching them a life lesson this way. One of the things I have seen when looking at the rituals and habits the top 1% parents teach their children, is that they always try to teach valuable life lessons. Teaching something of value over and over again, will have compounding effects on their lives.

Here is an example I read about a long time ago, a multimillionaire, most likely like a billionaire today, taught his two sons a lesson on how to protect their money. He would give them an allowance each every week and then he would work on getting the money back from them before the week was over, doing whatever it took. He believed this would be a very valuable lesson for them in the future. It took him a few years before he could no longer get the money back. Both sons became wealthy in their adult lives. Can you imagine if done right, what kind of world view the children will have when growing up, how will they see the world, if they are taught to protect their money like that? Can you imagine how simple the structure of business could possibly seem to them? I am not saying this is the right way, only sharing this as an example of a life lesson taught by a successful parent.

Bill and Melinda Gates give their children an allowance each week, but the children have to give one third of the money away. They can select who gets the money, but they have to give one third away, that is a must. Melinda and Bill take their children with them when they volunteer at their community and try to work with the charities that are close to their children's hearts. What do you think that teaches the children in the long run? What is the compounded effect on their lives? Will they become valuable contributors in society? I believe so. I also know that by giving you will start receiving.

COMPOUNDING EFFECTS IN YOUR LIFE AND YOUR CHILDREN'S LIVES ARE DUE TO RITUALS THAT TURN INTO HABITS DUE TO HARD WORK

There are no magic solutions. Almost every person who makes it, financially or otherwise, in life works hard to get there. More than half of the self-made millionaires today come from a humble background, not from wealth. You can reach your goals faster by guidance from a person who has done it before, but we are talking about the difference in years from now, not months. It will take time to get there, but with help you will achieve your goals sooner. The results from the first day you start compounding your life's efforts into a success story are most often not seen until years later.

The stories we hear about someone suddenly getting rich in a couple of months, are about persons who have spent years preparing to be in the position of being able to do that. I recently watched the documentary about Justin Bieber, the singer, and from the news it looked to me like this kid simply put one song on YouTube, someone noticed him, and he became rich and famous. I was glad to see that my perception of reality was correct once again and the perception of reality through news media was wrong again. Justin Bieber is very talented and started to show his talents at a very early age. He did more as an artist before the age of 14, than most people do in a lifetime. His success is no coincidence. The road to success is always the result of the compounded effects of good rituals and habits you have in your life.

If you decide to run 1 extra mile each week for the rest of your life and don't change anything else, you might not see the difference between you and your classmate with the same lifestyle until after 3-5 years. Imagine if you changed 10 little things in your life, you could be able to see the difference in 1-3 years from now. Your life is a marathon not a sprint. The same thing can be said about your children. The small things you decide to teach them as rituals, will start to compound in their lives right away and develop into great habits.

JOURNALING

Here is a way you can give yourself a great gift, a year from now. If you have a spouse, you can create a journal and each day write one sentence about your spouse, what you appreciate and find the positive in her/him. After a year give this journal to your spouse. It will probably be a great gift for your spouse, but the compounded effects of the journal will become your biggest gift to yourself, because the more you focus on the positive side of your spouse the more positivity comes into the relationship. This journal can be used to write about your children as well.

A gratitude exercise with your children, as a morning ritual for example, is something that will definitely compound positive results into your and your children's lives. Each day say out loud three things you are grateful for and ask your children to do the same. At a certain point it will feel as natural to do that, as brushing your teeth and it is a great way to start the day. I do that each time I wake up with my children.

TRACKING WHAT YOU DO

Tracking what you do is one of the things that help you implement rituals or to adjust your current habits. By tracking everything you do you can easily find what you need to change to attract better results in your life. This is simple, but at the same time, simple things are simple to forget or not to do at all. What goal is your priority, what long term goal with your children or yourself have you decided means the most to you and will give you the greatest return?

Let's say your goal is to make your children great at managing money. Record everything they spend their money on, if they are old enough then have them record it themselves.

> Do this in a simple manner with 4 columns on a piece of paper and each time they spend something, have them write down when they spent the money, what they spent it on, how much they spent, and finally ask them if it was necessary or unnecessary to spend that money, with the letter "N" or "U" in the fourth column.

> Have them do a summary on another page with three columns. First column is for the month and year, second column is for amount spent that month, and third column is for the label, necessary or unnecessary.

> This way it will be easy to monitor each month of the year if they are spending their money on things they consider necessary or not.

How much could they have saved if they did not spend any money on what they consider as unnecessary purchases? Make sure they sum up each month at the beginning of the following month. The children should catch on quickly, but of course it depends on their age. If they start when they are over 5 years of age it should not take long to understand how this works. I would make sure to mark all charities as necessary in the log, because we are teaching them, that giving to charity is a natural thing and part of prosperity. Knowing the more they give the more they receive. If your children is younger than five years old, you might have to account for things that you buy for the child, like gum, teddy bears or anything else he/she asks for and you buy. Regardless of the age, you can always find a way to start talking about how to spend your money wisely and how not to. Children are quick learners and they understand more than most of us give them credit for.

If you decide that the most value for your children is to think outside the box, then teach them to challenge everything they see. Teach them that one way is not necessarily the right way. Ask them if they think there is a better way of doing something they are doing, challenge their intellect and help them create new and better solutions. This is simple when they are using Lego's for example. If I see my youngest daughter doing something that could easily be done better, I always say to her; *"use your brain."* When I tell her this today, she knows exactly what it means so she steps back and thinks about it. If she can't figure it out she will ask me how. She has even caught me doing something that could be done better and said to me; *"dad you are not using your brain!"*

LEARN SOMETHING NEW EVERYDAY

A simple decision you can make, and will have massive compounding effects on your life, is to spend 20 minutes per day to learn something new, listen to audio books or read a book. You could use the time it takes you to commute to your job or school for this, knowing that it will change your marathon success run, that life is, in many ways. If you do something better by one tenth of one percent each day, you will be on a path to greatness. By increasing your income by one tenth of one percent each day on average, for example, you will increase it by one thousand percent ten years from now. Compounding effects are so amazing. With every little fraction of a percent you teach your children a new life skill or to do something better, you will see it multiplied in the future if you teach them to transform that into a habit.

CHANGING YOUR HABITS

The habits we adapt into our lives are what we become, the older the habit, the bigger the roots of the habit, just like a tree, and the more difficult it is to change it. For you as a parent it is very important to start working on changing the habits you know you do not want to condition developing into your children's lives. It is easier for us to teach our children new rituals because their habits are not old and it is pretty easy for them to undo them, before they create new routines and make it a lifelong habit.

Of course it is best to teach them rituals through leading by example, but sometimes we are teaching them a habit that does not fit into our own lives. Your child might have a musical talent for example, and you will help him/her to make a habit of nurturing that talent, regardless if you have any musical talents or not. This does not mean that you have to force yourself into learning to play an instrument. You could focus on your own talents during the time of day when your child is practicing, you could, for example, sit down and read for 30 minutes after dinner, and by making this a ritual or a habit you would be leading by example. Keep in mind that you can lead by example even if you are not doing the exact same thing as your children. In my opinion the more you can sync your habits to your children's habits, the easier it will become to help them stay on the path to create successful habits for life, and the easier it will be to watch the positive effects of that habit compound success in their lives and yours as well.

STICK TO YOUR ROUTINE

The biggest problem most people have is to stick to their routines long enough for them to become lifelong habits and start seeing the effects compounded into their success story. Your why is very important for your growth to compound over time. Many people have reached success but feel miserable because their why was only to accomplish that goal versus people that reach their goals with a powerful why as a fulfillment in their lives. Your why has to be more than the goal itself, to be able to sustain the success, it has to be greater than just being about you. Is your why strong enough? If I would lay a 40 feet long wood plank on the ground and offer you $20 to walk it, you would probably do it. If I would put the same plank 200 feet into the air and ask you to walk it there for $20, you would probably not, yet if the 40 foot plank was the only way you would save your children from a burning building you would not even have to think about it. Money cannot be your why, but on the other hand what can be done with purchasing power of money, can be a why. Your why has to be something that drives you on, that you have a passion for, so that you can implement the small changes into your life, long enough to reap the benefits of the compounded effects on your life through habits.

REDEFINE YOUR WHY TO MATCH YOUR CORE VALUES

Tony Robbins has emphasized that when you are looking for what really drives you, your why, you must also think about your core values in life. If your core values for example, are family, and you are creating a financial why that is important to you, but is so demanding that it drives you away from your family, you have a friction between your core values and your why. When you realize this is happening, you have to redefine your why to match your core values in life. The less friction we have the more likely we are to succeed making the journey smoother and the more meaningful as well. When setting your goals, make sure to focus on each aspect of your life. Keep the balance between your career, health, relationships, and your spiritualism. Write down the goals for it to work as a road map to get you there. Finally, track your journey in writing, adjusting the goals as you review your data over time. Remember that even though it might be hard work to track everything in the beginning, it gets easier. When your cash flow increases you can start to hire people to do this for you.

> "If you want to have more, you have to become more.
>
> For things to change, you have to change.
>
> For things to get better, you have to become better.
>
> If you improve, everything will improve for you.
>
> If you grow, your money will grow; your relationships, your health, your business and every external effect will mirror that growth in equal correlation."
>
> Jim Rohn

All your small changes compound into your life over time, and making a choice not to do something, is also a choice.

How much time are you spending on reading the news each day?

Can you decrease it by one percent each day for a three month period; can you spend less time feeding your brain negativity?

What about increasing the positivity you watch each day by one percent, do you think you could do that? If so, then simply swap out the negative time for positive time. If you spend 30 minutes per day watching news, or in other words negatively conditioning your views of your own reality by listening to experts who focus on negativity, then choose to use that time instead to feed your brain positive material.

Out of all the rituals and methods described in this book, how much difference do you think this single advice of swapping the negativity out for the positivity would make in your life?

It would make all the difference in the world, your reality would never be the same.

What small changes can you start making today as a person or as a parent, that will help you step into the identity or personality you need to be, to receive the success or reach the goals you desire? What small thing can you teach your children today that will compound into greatness after 20 years? Do you think it is not worth it because 20 years is a long time? If so, what reason do you need, so that you perceive the action today worth it? When you find the answer to this question you will have found your why, your reason to start implementing any small change into your children's lives today that will compound into greatness 20 years from now.

NO ARGUING

What is your goal? What are you striving for? Whatever you goal is, this simple advice will help you to reduce arguing or even eliminate it all together. When you are faced with a situation were you would normally start to nag or complain, think about what that situation has to do with your goal? If, for example, you argue with your spouse about putting things down where they are not supposed to be, then ask yourself next time before wasting time and energy, whether this thing or situation has any meaning for you goal in life. If it does not change the end results, then don't bother arguing about it. Don't waist your time and energy arguing about things that do not affect your goals in life, because if you do, then you are actually taking one step further away from your goal.

BAD HABITS

If there is a habit you have right now, but want to quit doing, start by asking yourself if you can swap the habit out for something else? Let's say you want to swap out your after dinner sweet tooth for example. Today you might choose to eat ice cream after dinner, which might be around 1.000 – 1.500 calories in addition to your dinner. You could replace it with a piece of a healthy dark cocoa chocolate, it might be enough to fulfill your sweet tooth cravings and as long as you don't change anything else the 1.500 calories compounded over time might be your key to a healthy and long life.

It is incredible how much difference you can make in your life by changing one habit. Imagine if you would set your goals to change 5, or even 10 habits in the next 12 months. You could list each habit on your calendar, explaining when you are going to change it and how you will do it, if you know. Adding a morning ritual each day where you do mindset work, read, or listen to positive inspiring authors, is one of the small changes that will make a big difference over time.

Even though most people like baby steps and gradually working on the changes in their lives you might be part of the smaller group of people who like jumping into the cold water, meaning you might want to decide to change your lifestyle dramatically overnight. You know yourself better than anyone else, you know what suits you the best, how you are most likely to keep at it, not quitting. There are some people who change overnight and that might be you, but if you are like most of us, then small changes are the right way to make your transformation smooth and lasting.

One key thing about changing bad habits is to focus on the new positive habits you have chosen. Remember that you should not focus on the habits you can't or won't do anymore, because then you will attract them back into your life. If your habit was to snack between meals and instead you decided to drink water, you could select different kinds of water, one day with this flavor, and the next day a new flavor, focusing on what you are going to try out instead of focusing on the snacks you are no longer eating. The first step is always the hardest, but when you get through the first phase, the next phase will be so much easier. The lucky get luckier, the successful get more successful, we have all heard this before. It is what is called momentum. Once you start these changes you will experience what is called the snowball effect or compounding the results from the first phase and then the next and so forth.

SUMMARY

Any ritual or habit you decide to adapt or change today, however small, will compound over time.

By increasing your income by one tenth of a percent each day you will create a 1,000% increase over the next 10 years.

When you decide to teach your children a new ritual that will become their lifelong habit, try to visualize how it will impact them compounded 10 years from now.

Try to keep in mind, each time you slack off and a new habit fades out or you simply decide to stop doing that new ritual before it becomes a habit, how this will compound in 10 years from now in your life?

Focus as much a possible on the positive changes in your life.

Good habits give the household stability.

Good sleeping habits can lead to more romantic nights for the parents, or more me-time.

Your child learns about her/his own space and gains a sense of independence by sleeping in her/his own bed.

Stable sleep is one of the key factors to healthy growth and maturity for a child, and your child will develop a better mood.

The more you are aware of your habits the more stable your schedule becomes, and the easier it is to change your habits.

Your child will feel better with good life long habits.

You will feel better with good habits for life.

IN CLOSING

Firstly I want to congratulate you on taking action, getting this book, reading it and implementing new routines into your life. Everything we do in life starts with a thought. You had a thought that led you to the point of reading this book. You have taken the initiative on your journey to personal growth and you are including your children as well. Well done!

The world's best transmitter and receiver for frequency, is your mind. You influence your children by the frequency of energy you live in, and they learn not only from what you tell them and show them, but even more from the frequency you are transmitting. You must learn to be grateful for today and each day finding the positive things in life, expressing your gratitude for those things. Step into the identity you really want, **TODAY**, and live like all your dreams are already realized.

The methods and rituals discussed in this book are not carved into stone so to speak, I even encourage you to adjust and adapt these rituals how it fits best into your family environment. You may use the information in this book how it best suits you, you can teach your children and you may use the content as your own in your own words. I am not the inventor of these methods, I am only the messenger who has brought together information from some of the most successful people on the planet, I have merely put them into plain terms and adjusted some of the methods for parents to be able to teach their children how to become the best generation yet. The process of self-improvement is often hard but most of the time fun and exciting. Enjoy the time you spend teaching this to your children. Remember that when you start to teach this material the better you will become at it yourself. It is something I learned while working as a teacher at the University of Akureyri, Iceland, I already knew the material but it was first when I started teaching it, that I truly got it myself.

Now that you have spent time reading this book, make sure to implement as much as possible, but you don't have to do it all at once, start by implementing something new into your daily rituals **TODAY** and see what changes lay ahead. I know you will be pleasantly surprised to see how your child will soak in the material like a sponge.

What grabbed your attention first time reading the book?

Was it to teach your child a gratitude ritual each day?

Or was it to teach your child how to manifest their dream into reality?

Maybe it was to teach them about charity and giving, by letting them participate in making someone else's life better or helping you in volunteering for a cause?

Will you pick out tasks for your children to give them cognitive challenges and developing their brain functionality?

Are you willing to try intermittent fasting once a week were the family only drinks water for 12-18 hours, changing their metabolism and developing ketones for the brain?

Will you encourage your children to play sports?

Maybe the practice of having three piggy banks sounds like a good idea to start with, teaching your children how to divide money into, fun money, charity money, and savings?

Are you going to teach your children how to raise their frequency by changing their attitude and about the effects positive energy has on the body and soul?

What anchoring techniques will you implement knowingly to trigger a positive response in your children?

Did it catch your attention to teach your children to eliminate words like can't, won't, naah, no, impossible, and other words that limit their thoughts and actions?

Maybe you want to start with one small thing today and see it compound into their lives with repetition and persistence?

Will you teach your children to be in alignment with their goals and to be in the right state of vibration of receiving their desired goals, by focusing on the goals, thinking positive thoughts and raising their vibrational frequency into alignment with their goals?

FOCUS ON YOUR GOALS

If you put all your focus on your thumb for example and keep it there for a while you will start to notice things in your thumb, you don't even have to have your eyes open. Focus long enough and you will even feel your heartbeat in your thumb. It is amazing how you start to feel and see new perspective of such a simple thing like your thumb, just by keeping your focus on it. Like always, I encourage you to try it, set your alarm 3 minutes from now, close your eyes and just focus on your thumb, the whole time, can you do it? Don't take my word for it, try it yourself and find out for yourself, there is nothing like experiencing things for yourself. This is true about anything you focus on, and this is why we say that everything you focus on will grow. Focusing on abundance and health in your life as well in your children's lives will do the same thing. You start to notice new things and new feelings regarding your growth together.

This book is merely a humble introduction to the rituals and methods we can implement into our lives and by reading it you have opened up your eyes to the endless possibilities that lay ahead for you and your children. My wish is to enrich the lives of families all over the globe, bring them together and build a foundation for them to reach every dream they can possible think of. I wish to see as many parents as possible implementing as much as possible into their lives and grow rich with happiness and fulfillment. This book is the foundation of the **Watchon** brand which strives to teach parents easy, simple methods to implement and provide entertainment to children with a message that will help them flourish. The entertainment and teaching materials are brought to the children through mobile applications (all free to use and safe for children with no links leading them out to the internet), music videos, interactive stories (where the children make a decision on how the story unfolds, teaching them to learn from their mistakes and others as well) and in the near future, TV episodes teaching them life lessons through entertainment.

I cannot thank you enough; you are the reason why I devote my time and energy to making this world a little bit better for those who choose it, for themselves and their children.

Huni Hunfjord.

LEARN MORE ABOUT HUNI HUNFJORD

http://amazon.com/author/HuniHunfjord

http://HuniHunfjord.com

http://IcyDesign.com

Learn more about the Watchon Brand

http://Watchon.Club

Learn more about Focus Gym ♡♡ Be you!

http://FocusGymBeyou.com

ABOUT THE AUTHOR

Huni Hunfjord is the author of Sleeping Habits and Routines, Top 1% Parents Raise Top 1% Children, The Mentorian, Our Road without Boundaries and Founder of the Watchon brand and Focus Gym ♡♡ Be you! As a father of three, children and entrepreneurship are core to his life. Huni loves creating apps, music videos, new ventures, coaching and interactive stories centered around children that parents can use to help them grow and develop into the best possible version of themselves. This book has been created for parents to inspire their children by setting an example for them and including them in the process.

OTHER BOOKS BY HUNI HUNFJORD

Sleeping Habits and Routines

The Mentorian

Our Road without Boundaries

ONE LAST THING...

If you enjoyed this book or found it useful I'd be very grateful if you'd post a short review on Amazon. Your support really does make a difference and I read all the reviews personally so I can get your feedback and make this book even better.

If you'd like to leave a review all you need to do is to go and review this book on Amazon here;

http://amazon.com/author/HuniHunfjord

or,

if you have purchased a printed copy of the book, send your review directly to testimonial@HuniHunfjord.com as we would love to include your review on our website.

Thanks again for your support, you are awesome!

Huni Hunfjord.

www.ingramcontent.com/pod-product-compliance
Lightning Source LLC
Chambersburg PA
CBHW060953230426
43665CB00015B/2182